VOLUME 11

PROVERBS ECCLESIASTES and SONG OF SOLOMON

Frank Johnson

ABINGDON PRESS
Nashville

This book is printed on recycled, acid-free paper.

Library of Congress Cataloging-in-Publication Data

Cokesbury basic Bible commentary.
    Basic Bible commentary / by Linda B. Hinton . . . [et al.].
        p. cm.
    Originally published: Cokesbury basic Bible commentary. Nashville: Graded Press, © 1988.
    ISBN 0-687-02620-2 (pbk. : v. 1 : alk. paper)
    1. Bible—Commentaries. I. Hinton, Linda B. II. Title.
[BS491.2.C65   1994]
220.7—dc20   94-10965
                                                                                                          CIP

ISBN 0-687-02630-X (v. 11, Proverbs–Song of Solomon)
ISBN 0-687-02620-2 (v. 1, Genesis)
ISBN 0-687-02621-0 (v. 2, Exodus–Leviticus)
ISBN 0-687-02622-9 (v. 3, Numbers–Deuteronomy)
ISBN 0-687-02623-7 (v. 4, Joshua–Ruth)
ISBN 0-687-02624-5 (v. 5, 1–2 Samuel)
ISBN 0-687-02625-3 (v. 6, 1–2 Kings)
ISBN 0-687-02626-1 (v. 7, 2 Chronicles)
ISBN 0-687-02627-X (v. 8, Ezra–Esther)
ISBN 0-687-02628-8 (v. 9, Job)
ISBN 0-687-02629-6 (v. 10, Psalms)
ISBN 0-687-02631-8 (v. 12, Isaiah)
ISBN 0-687-02632-6 (v. 13, Jeremiah–Lamentation)
ISBN 0-687-02633-4 (v. 14, Ezekiel–Daniel)
ISBN 0-687-02634-2 (v. 15, Hosea–Jonah)
ISBN 0-687-02635-0 (v. 16, Micah–Malachi)
ISBN 0-687-02636-9 (v. 17, Matthew)
ISBN 0-687-02637-7 (v. 18, Mark)
ISBN 0-687-02638-5 (v. 19, Luke)
ISBN 0-687-02639-3 (v. 20, John)
ISBN 0-687-02640-7 (v. 21, Acts)
ISBN 0-687-02642-3 (v. 22, Romans)
ISBN 0-687-02643-1 (v. 23, 1–2 Corinthians)
ISBN 0-687-02644-X (v. 24, Galatians–Ephesians)
ISBN 0-687-02645-8 (v. 25, Philippians–2 Thessalonians)
ISBN 0-687-02646-6 (v. 26, 1 Timothy–Philemon)
ISBN 0-687-02647-4 (v. 27, Hebrews)
ISBN 0-687-02648-2 (v. 28, James–Jude)
ISBN 0-687-02649-0 (v. 29, Revelation)
ISBN 0-687-02650-4 (complete set of 29 vols.)

01 02 03 — 10 9 8 7 6 5 4

MANUFACTURED IN THE UNITED STATES OF AMERICA

Contents

Outline

Proverbs

I. A Father's Instruction (1:1–4:27)
  A. Superscription (1:1)
  B. The Purpose of Proverbs (1:2-7)
  C. Avoiding the Ways of Sinners (1:8-19)
  D. Wisdom's Prophetic Announcement (1:20-33)
  E. The Benefits of Wisdom (2:1-22)
  F. The Benefits of Faith (3:1-12)
  G. Wisdom and God (3:13-20)
  H. Moral Instruction (3:21-35)
  I. A Father's Instruction (4:1-27)
II. Moral Values of the Wise (5:1–9:18)
  A. Avoiding temptations from women (5:1-23)
  B. Instructions against wrong conduct (6:1-35)
  C. Instructions to avoid adultery (7:1-27)
  D. Wisdom's second announcement (8:1-36)
  E. Wisdom and Folly contrasted (9:1-18)
III. The Proverbs of Solomon (10:1–22:16)
  A. Group one (10:1-32)
  B. Group two (11:1-31)
  C. Group three (12:1-28)
  D. Group four (13:1-25)
  E. Group five (14:1-35)
  F. Group six (15:1-33)
  G. Group seven (16:1-33)

H. Group eight (17:1-28)
I. Group nine (18:1-24)
J. Group ten (19:1-29)
K. Group eleven (20:1-30)
L. Group twelve (21:1-31)
M. Group thirteen (22:1-16)
IV. The Words of the Wise (22:17–24:34)
   A. Introduction (22:17-21)
   B. Thirty sayings 22:22–24:22
   C. Further sayings of the wise (24:23-34)
V. The Proverbs of Solomon (25:1–29:27)
VI. Further Instruction (30:1–31:31)
   A. The words of Agur (30:1-9)
   B. Instructions and numerical sayings (30:10-33)
   C. The words of Lemuel (31:1-9)
   D. The ideal wife (31:10-31)

Ecclesiastes

I. Qoheleth's Quest for Meaning (1:1–3:22)
   A. Superscription (1:1)
   B. Vanity of vanities (1:2-11)
   C. Search for meaning and value (1:12–2:26)
   D. Times and seasons (3:1-15)
   E. Human mortality and divine justice (3:16-22)
II. Practical Moral Teaching (4:1–8:17)
   A. Social injustice (4:1-3)
   B. Better this than that (4:4-16)
   C. Miscellaneous observations (5:1-20)
   D. More vanities on earth (6:1-12)
   E. Wisdom and the wise (7:1-29)
   F. The plight of human finitude (8:1-17)
III. The Realities of Existence (9:1–12:14)
   A. One fate comes to all (9:1-3)
   B. Life is superior to death (9:4-10)
   C. Time and chance (9:11-12)
   D. Wisdom's limited value (9:13-18)

Introduction to Wisdom

Proverbs, Job, and Ecclesiastes belong to a particular group of books within the Hebrew Bible commonly known as the Wisdom Literature. Members of the Roman Catholic community add two additional wisdom books to their biblical canon, Sirach and the Wisdom of Solomon. The early church included Psalms and Song of Solomon among the poetical books of the Old Testament, bringing the number to seven.

The designation of these books as *Wisdom Literature* stems from the central theme of these writings, namely the theme of wisdom as the goal of all human activity. Wisdom, or being wise, refers to several different kinds of knowledge or expertise that may be achieved in different ways and may be exhibited in diverse forms. Accordingly, the wisdom books appear quite different in literary styles, ethical values, and theological themes.

The final versions seem to have been the literary product of a special class of persons in early Israel, known as the *sages* or *wise men*. This professional group spent considerable energy discovering the meaning and values of human existence within a divine moral order. They also collected, organized, and wrote down the adages and proverbial lore of previous generations.

Human existence, as perceived by the sage, is comprehensible only within the limits of wisdom. Happiness and well-being come only to the persons who discover and exercise wisdom. The literary results of these practical insights into life and its meaning come down to us in the Wisdom Literature of the Old Testament.

What Does Wisdom Mean?

The Hebrew term for wisdom is *hokmah*. Across the many centuries of ancient Israelite history, this term amassed a broad range of meanings, so many in fact that a single simple definition is almost impossible to formulate. Generally, wisdom may be said to refer to five types of human activities: (1) technical skill, (2) political insight, (3) moral knowledge, (4) a gift of divine revelation, and (5) superior knowledge, broadly speaking. Probably it is best not to assume an evolutionary pattern of historical growth for the concept of wisdom, since many of these different meanings probably functioned simultaneously in early Israel.

First, the term *wisdom* is applied to persons who exhibit expert technical skill in some area of craftsmanship or construction. In Exodus 35:30-35, Bezalel, a wise craftsman filled with God's Spirit, is adept at working with gold, silver, bronze, and with stones. Similarly, Oholiab has extraordinary talent with fabrics. Elsewhere other persons highly skilled in some technical vocation are identified as wise: farmers (Isaiah 28:23-29), professional mourners (Jeremiah 9:17), and entrepreneurs (Ezekiel 28:4-5).

Verification of the wisdom of these persons came by the empirical method; firsthand experience and direct observation validated their wisdom. While Bezalel's skill is clearly the result of long experience and training, the capacity for this expertise is viewed by the biblical writer as a gift from God. Thus a secular talent was not distinguished from a theological interpretation.

Second, wisdom is also used to characterize persons who provided astute political advice. Ahithophel, a trusted political adviser to King David who turned traitor to participate in Absalom's ill-fated revolt, is considered wise (2 Samuel 16–23). An anonymous wise woman from Tekoa aids Joab in convincing David to recall his son Absalom from exile (2 Samuel 14:1-20). Certainly this political astuteness applied to King Solomon as well (1 Kings 4:29).

Third, a wise person is one with keen moral insight (Proverbs 1:2). These persons have knowledge of the divinely established pattern of cause and effect, and such knowledge clearly enables them to attain worldly success and to avoid the disasters of folly. The particular values associated with this moral insight enable a person to achieve happiness and to prosper materially in this life. These virtues can be learned, but must be taught too, since they are not altogether natural. In a word, wisdom morality is an ethic that relies on human reason and moral effort to master the game of life. It has a definite utilitarian nature and determines moral worth on the basis of consequences.

The entire value system and the means of achieving it have a definite theological foundation in the notions of Creation theology and the concept of the fear of the Lord. Both of these themes will be discussed further in a later chapter; it is sufficient here to stress that morality was never viewed as an end in itself, nor held apart from religious faith. The ultimate purpose of right conduct was to satisfy a person's obligation to God. Moral right was right only because God declared it to be right.

Fourth, in Proverbs 1:20-33 and 9:1-6 the concept of wisdom is personified and depicted as a female prophet. She boldly extends the Lord's gift of life to those who respond affirmatively to her call, and utters God's judgment upon all who shun her counsel. Wisdom is understood here too as the gift of divine revelation, only here the idea is personified and depicted as a darling child, playing as God creates the world.

Finally, wisdom is used to designate a broader, more inclusive quality than denoted by the four preceding

special abilities, namely superior knowledge. King
Solomon (1 Kings 4:29-34) serves as the prime model for
such a wise person in the Old Testament. The
tremendous breadth of his knowledge ranged from
judicial matters to zoology, from moral conduct to
literary genius. Apart from moral excellence or even the
religious element in wisdom as God's gift, a wise person
in the Old Testament is the person who is simply smarter
than the average individual—smarter in every way.

The Theology of Wisdom Literature

As we examine Proverbs, Ecclesiastes, and Song of
Solomon, it will become clear at once that the theological
realm operative for the sage differs remarkably from that
found in the Pentateuch, the historical books, and the
prophets. Even within the Old Testament itself, notably
Jeremiah 18:18 and Ezekiel 7:26, attention is called to the
differences among the priest, the prophet, and the sage.
The *torah* or instruction of the priest as well as the word
of the prophet both reflect a belief that divine revelation
somehow was not a part of the natural order of things,
and often intruded into history. God and nature were
related as Creator and created, but even so, sharp
differences still existed between them. And Israel's
history, in particular as interpreted by Israel's historians,
was understandable only from a theological point of
view—history and revelation.

By contrast, the sage's world lay in the realm of
concrete human experience and individual ethical values
as means to a happy, successful life. Formal religious
practices and priestly torah were part of another world
for the sage. Even the word of the prophet fell outside
the sage's sphere of operation. For the person of wisdom,
divine revelation came through a moral order open to
reason, experience, and reflection. For every human
action, there was an obvious consequence. Successful

living came about precisely because a person knew this pattern and operated within its limits.

Since this moral system had been established by God, faith became the keen awareness of this order, indeed a profound respect (fear of the Lord) for its operations. Reason and human experience were fully capable of perceiving and understanding the will of God. No special instruction or divinely inspired word were necessary. The sage lived in a different world, and his literary expressions stand in bold relief to the work of priests, prophets, and historians.

From Whence Did Wisdom Come?

Across the long years of her national history, Israel witnessed the rise and development of three classes of religious leaders: the priest, the prophet, and the wise man or sage (see Jeremiah 18:18). Each of these three groups communicated God's words in distinctive ways. The priest issued law or instruction, the prophet spoke oracles of judgment or salvation, and the sage offered counsel. Many scholars now believe that the sages were a professional class in Israel, and that much of our biblical Wisdom Literature derives from their work, either directly or indirectly.

The sages seem to have been a learned class of persons who were highly regarded for their practical and perceptive insights into morality, politics, and psychology. They produced an elitist code of ethics (now found in Proverbs) that assumed a high level of economic well-being and social development. The values they promoted were aimed at self-actualization and happiness through obedience to the divinely established moral order. Highly individualistic and utilitarian, the sages concerned themselves with how persons could best succeed in society as it existed at that time and how they could best transmit the wisdom.

However, not all the Wisdom Literature originated

with these learned sages in the national state during the monarchy. The beginnings of this kind of knowledge dated far back into the early stages of Israelite history. Many of the proverbial sayings later collected by the sages first began as folklore, as riddles, and as pithy sayings told for amusement as well as for erudition.

Cultures throughout the world claim long literary histories for proverbs. Perhaps such sayings were passed along for generations from parent to child, or by singers of tales. Clearly, the imperative-style instructional material originated in the family unit, with the father taking primary responsibility for his child's moral education. In capsulating these fundamental insights of nature and of human behavior into literary forms, the ancient Israelites carefully nurtured a tradition of proverbs that eventually became a part of a body of material preserved and enriched by the sages. It is entirely possible that some of the sayings of the Old Testament date back to these early periods.

Yet a third source for the Old Testament wisdom material was the theological community in ancient Israel. Whether or not such persons in the community were vocationally distinctive, or were perhaps even sages, cannot be determined. But many Israelite proverbs bear an unmistakable religious imprint (10:22). Such sayings reflect a deep faith in God as the moral force in human society.

Other sayings attest to divine guidance in the affairs of persons (Proverbs 16:9). But perhaps the most telling evidence that secular wisdom was closely related to Israelite faith is the crucial declaration that the fear of the Lord is the beginning of wisdom (Proverbs 1:7). At precisely what point in Israelite history these sayings underwent this immersion in theology is uncertain. It is also difficult to identify the social circles or institutions out of which the proverbs came. Perhaps some sages who experienced their moral teachings through two-line proverbial sayings also expressed their faith through the same literary form.

The majority of proverbial sayings and other longer pieces within the Wisdom Literature originated from within these three circles. Even so, King Solomon must be mentioned also in any discussion of sources for wisdom. Whether he penned as many proverbs himself as mentioned in 1 Kings 4:32, or whether he patronized learned sages in some type of royal school, Solomon must be credited with bringing Israelite wisdom into prominence.

With King Solomon, wisdom became the special province of the royal court. Training and instruction passed from the home to the school; the style became didactic and the tone persuasive. Certainly, as Israelite culture flourished under the monarchy, a new pride grew in the human intellect. Thus the coming of age marked the real birth of the professional sage.

Introduction to Proverbs

The book of Proverbs presents a wide range of moral instructions, dressed in the literary styles of proverbial sayings and brief poems. The six sections within the book were written over many centuries, by many hands, and under vastly different circumstances. But beneath the watchful eye of post-exilic editors, these many diverse sayings were assembled, edited, and offered confidently as a guide to a happy, fulfilling, and prosperous life.

The Content of Proverbs

The range of ethical teachings is as broad as human experience itself. This anthology presents advice on conduct such as proper sexual behavior, industriousness, effective communication, loyalty, friendship, and abstinence from intoxicants.

Many sayings reflect a strong religious belief, encouraging faith and obedience to the Lord's will. Yet other sayings probe the mysteries of God's revelations in the strange world of nature or within the perplexing nexus of human relationships. Some sayings reflect the regularity and predictability of the natural order. All these sayings are preserved precisely because they work well, because they have been tested in the vast crucible of human experience, and because they have all stood the test of time. They present a high standard of conduct. The writers are confident in their belief that God rewards the righteous person and punishes the evildoer.

Certainly the book of Proverbs is a manual of

instruction, but even more, it is a profound synthesis of early faith and human reason. For the sages who coined the proverbs and edited the sayings comprising Proverbs, there was no greater act of piety than the apprehension and enactment of moral virtue. The goal of moral knowledge was an instrumental goal, useful in conforming to God's will as exhibited in the natural and moral order. The book of Proverbs is a fitting legacy to this very different model of religious faith. Moral conduct was indeed an appropriate expression of faith in God.

Structure and Organization

The book of Proverbs can be divided into six sections, based on internal headings and clear changes in literary style and ethical/religious content: (1) Introduction (1:1–9:18); (2) The Proverbs of Solomon (10:1–22:16); (3) The Sayings of the Wise (22:17–24:22); (4) Supplement to the Sayings of the Wise (24:23-34); (5) The Proverbs of Solomon-II (25:1–29:27); and (6) Four Appendices (30:1–31:31). Analysis of these sections suggests to scholars that Proverbs consists of various strands of material that originally existed independently of one another. Variations in literary style alone indicate separate authors, different settings and dates, and distinct purposes. For these reasons, Proverbs has aptly been characterized as an anthology.

Just as one finds no transitional elements between the six separate sections, other than the superscript headings, there is little effort made to link or group individual sayings within respective units. Especially in 10:1–22:16, this style can lead to a certain monotony.

Authorship and Date

Tradition ascribes principal authorship of the book of Proverbs to King Solomon, the son of David, King of Israel. In part, this belief is based on the superscriptions in the book itself (1:1, 10:1, and 25:1). Also, Solomon is alleged to have composed three thousand proverbs (1 Kings 4:29-34), numerous songs, and to have been wise in greater measure than the sands of the seashore. However, as we indicated earlier, internal literary divisions and subject analysis suggest that many persons composed the sayings and poems in Proverbs. In fact, even Proverbs itself mentions the authors Agur (30:1) and Lemuel (31:1). Still other sayings were collected by the men of Hezekiah (25:1).

While King Solomon could easily have written and collected thousands of proverbs (since he was probably responsible for promoting and nurturing the wisdom tradition in his royal court), the style, vocabulary, and theme of many sayings in chapters 1–9, 22:17–24:22, and 30–31 indicate authors and dates other than King Solomon. Yet because of Solomon's undisputed contributions to Israelite wisdom, the compilers of the Hebrew Bible were proper in honoring Solomon by the dedicatory superscription in 1:1.

The authorship of proverbial sayings stemmed from three major centers: the Royal Wisdom School (founded by Solomon and nurtured during the monarchy), folk tradition, and the theological community. Still other sayings arose from anonymous individuals in ancient Israel, and became part of an ever-increasing repository of collective knowledge available to the community. Also, we believe that a Hebrew sage borrowed substantial material from the Egyptian source known as *Instructions of Amenemope*. And from within the book of Proverbs, we have the materials ascribed to Agur (30:1) and Lemuel (31:1).

Because of the very nature of proverbial sayings as true and universal insight into human existence, they truly became the property of the entire community. The legacy of Proverbs is not, therefore, a legacy of a particular scribe or king, but the legacy of an entire nation. Proverbs is a true anthology of the ancient Israelite wisdom tradition.

The problem of assigning dates to either individual sayings or the collections of sayings is also difficult. Careful study of comparative Wisdom Literature from Egypt, Mesopotamia, and Ugarit has led Old Testament scholars to rethink earlier notions about the dating of certain literary forms and themes. A post-exilic date for Proverbs 1–9, for example, is no longer a necessary conclusion; there are parallel materials that are clearly from the tenth or ninth centuries.

Scholars also no longer maintain the notion that the two-line proverbial saying is a later development (or corruption) of the one-line unit. Further complicating the dating issue is the absence of specific historical references. As indicated earlier, the superscriptions are more reflective of special patronage than of actual Solomonic authorship. The difficulties of dating notwithstanding, the meaning of most proverbial sayings is relatively clear and timeless.

Although it is likely that most of the six sections of Proverbs were in existence by the latter part of the fourth century, differences in the arrangement of certain sections of Proverbs in the Greek translation of the Old Testament suggest that the book itself was not finalized until the late Hellenistic period. It is also entirely possible that a few sayings were added during that late phase of development, as suggested by Aramaic and Greek loan words.

Theological Themes in Proverbs

The book of Proverbs pivots on the axis of five major theological themes: (1) divine retribution, (2) the fear of the Lord, (3) moral conduct, (4) divine revelation, and (5) creation orders. Many other theological themes surface in Proverbs as well, as is to be expected in such an eclectic work. From time to time, certain themes may even appear to contradict one another. There are repetitions of themes, comparisons, contrasts, analogies, puns, and so forth. But most of the proverbs relate to the five themes mentioned above.

Divine retribution is the idea that the Lord blesses (rewards) the person of faith and righteousness, and punishes the apostate person and the evildoer. A detailed analysis of appropriate Old Testament texts reflects variation in both the means of retribution and the timing of a divine response. For example, in Genesis 18:22-33, because God is just (righteous), Abraham can persuade God to consider carefully judgment against Sodom. Even so, once Lot and his family escape, Sodom is destroyed; retribution is directly executed by God and is relatively swift. Elsewhere, in Habakkuk, God admonishes the prophet to *wait* and have faith (Habakkuk 2:3). The editor of the extended historical works in Deuteronomy through 2 Kings clearly feels that the Exile is a just punishment for Israel because of their apostasy. Isaiah and Jeremiah both view "history" as the realm where God operates.

While theological refinements indicate differences in the ways and means of retribution, the Old Testament most certainly views both history and nature as locales where the Lord rewards the righteous and punishes the evildoers. In Proverbs, however, divine retribution occurs through the operation of the moral order (11:8, 11). The law of act-consequence operates without exception: Evil acts bring their own punishment (1:8-19). Of course, this innate moral system of the universe is the creation of God, and as such it surely operates under God's will. But retribution for the sages does not involve suspensions of the ordinary scheme of nature or intrusion into history. Each human act contains intrinsically the seeds of its own consequence; this is retribution for the sage.

The *fear of the* LORD is an expression used by the sage to

refer to religious faith. In fact, for the sage, the ultimate level of human knowledge or insight brings a person to an acute consciousness of God's natural and social order. Human reason always requires the empowering of faith to function properly. Just as the natural order is governed by certain laws (such as gravity and inertia), so too is the social or moral order governed by act-consequence. The dangers occurring from ignoring this "order" of things are clear and foreboding. But the benefits of wisdom are success and fulfillment. True respect for this sovereign moral order of the universe is known as the fear of the Lord.

Logically following from the notion of the fear of the Lord is a strongly rigid moral code. The panoply of ethical values displayed in Proverbs was encoded into the universe by God. Therefore, conformity yields success! Right behavior, as prescribed by the divine moral order, brings prosperity, and vice versa. Thus morality for the sage was measured by consequences; utility became the guide to what God expected. Specifically, the sages warn against association with evil companions (1:8-19), consorting with harlots (7:10-23), drunkenness (23:29-35), and so forth. They commend industry, proper communication, etiquette, honesty, friendship, and above all, the fear of the Lord.

Fourth, the sages perceived God's presence in ways that were different from the concepts of revelation advanced by priests and prophets. The sages began, theologically, at a different point in their quest for divine knowledge; they began with general human experience in nature, and moved analogically to the realm of human morality. They observed the orderly operations of nature: the regular seasons, gravity, growth, mating patterns, and so forth. By analogy, human interrelationships exhibited similar patterns of predictability, because the same divine laws of act-consequence that animated nature also structured human existence. The will of the

Lord was clearly evident in the created order. Righteousness, loyalty, and prudence were God's moral expectations as preserved in experience.

Fifth, Creation for the sages assumes a different theological meaning from that of two of the authors of the Pentateuch, the Priestly and the Jahwist writers. Creation in Proverbs marks the establishment of both a natural and a moral order. It does not provide a historical framework for human sin and divine redemption. Creation here means regularity, predictability, causation, comprehensibility. Creation reflects the moral nature of the universe; the world and human existence are not indifferent moral concerns, precisely because God implanted a moral fabric within the scheme of the universe. To discover Creation is to discover God's moral will. The notion of divine Creation is a resounding affirmation of the meaning of human existence; life has value because God created it so.

Proverbs 1–4

Introduction to These Chapters

Superscription (1:1)

The Hebrew word *mashal*, usually translated *proverb*, refers to several different literary forms, as evidenced in verses 2-6, not just the two-line poetical sayings. The conceptual meaning of the term, however, is less clear. Some scholars suggest that *mashal* connotes a type of extraordinarily powerful word, that is a *winged word* that pierces to the very heart of reality. Other scholars believe that the origin of the word lies in the idea of comparison or similarity; that is, a proverb indicates a relationship of likeness between something known and something unknown. It stands to reason, however, that the language and literary forms used by the sages must have conveyed the awesome power of their pristine insights. Whether expressed as a folk saying (1 Samuel 24:13; 2 Samuel 5:8;

Jeremiah 31:29), as a riddle (Judges 14:14; Ezekiel 17:2), or as a proverbial saying (Proverbs 10:1–22:16), the *mashal* carried much weight in the mind of an ancient Israelite. Quite possibly, an aura of magic surrounded this word, as in an oath or a curse.

As indicated earlier in the Introduction to Wisdom, it is likely that the entire wisdom tradition received a tremendous impetus during the administration of King Solomon (967–925 B.C.). With an expanding governmental bureaucracy, Solomon found himself in need of highly trained technical personnel. Also, his diplomatic efforts broadened the already expanding intellectual vistas of tenth-century Israel. A new self-consciousness of humankind emerged, and new confidence in God's trust in humans prompted exploration into new areas of knowledge formerly thought to be off-limits. Solomon's reign in Jerusalem was truly a new day in Israel. Also, Solomon himself was the author of many proverbs and poems (1 Kings 4:32). His wisdom in all areas was recognized and respected by many nations (1 Kings 4:29). Thus it is perfectly appropriate that this superscription bears his name. As a title for the entire book, *The Proverbs of Solomon* lends authority and prestige and pays honor to the patron sage of wisdom.

The Purpose of Proverbs (1:2-7)

These six verses introduce not only chapters 1–9 but also the entire book with a clear statement of didactic purpose: This book is a manual of moral instruction. Rote memory, although obviously presumed, is secondary to personal embodiment of these teachings into one's own personal code of conduct and pattern of behavior. Persons of all ages, all levels of understanding, indeed all vocations, including the wise man, can learn and grow from studying this material. Mention is made of some of the literary forms in which these instructions are transmitted: a proverb, a figure, words of the wise, and riddles. These literary types are all indigenous to the wisdom tradition in Israel and elsewhere. The message of the entire introductory section is clarified and made precise through the use of parallelism: To know wisdom and instruction parallels understanding words of insight; prudence given to the simple parallels knowledge and discretion imparted to youth, and so forth. The value of positive repetition and reinforcement was well-known then, just as it is known today among educators.

In climactic style, these opening purposes point upward to morality, described in verse 3 as *righteousness, justice and equity* in the NRSV; or as *acquiring a disciplined and prudent life and doing what is right and just and fair* in the NIV, and most important to faith, to *the fear of the* LORD. This fear is, of course, not a sense of fright, but rather a profound respect for the divinely created moral order of the universe. It is an acute awareness of the structures of laws by means of which the world operates. Yet intellectual knowledge and moral behavior are not ends in themselves, but are means to achieve devout faith. To reach this sense of God's presence is surely the purpose of all knowledge. Morality is an expression of religious faith, and ultimately the study of Proverbs leads a reasonable person to faith in the Lord.

Avoiding the Ways of Sinners (1:8-19)

In a style similar to the royal instruction literature from ancient Egypt, Proverbs 1:8-19 is an admonition to refrain from the ways of sinners. The following structure suggests a development from a basic one-time prohibition (verse 10) to a larger unit, complete with motive clauses, the temptations of quick wealth, and consequences of wicked conduct.

Introduction (verses 8-9)
Admonition to avoid evil companions (verse 10)
The temptations of the evil ones (verses 11-14)
Repeat of initial admonition (verse 15)

The fate of evildoers (consequences) (verses 16-18)
Conclusion: Death comes from violence (verse 19)
The introduction (verses 8-9) sets the tone for the entire unit as didactic. Although the family unit was the principal setting for most moral education in ancient Israel, the specific references to family members—son, father, mother—are probably more stylistic than actual. The *instruction* of the father refers to strict, highly rigorous moral regulations. The *teaching* of the mother is more general, and perhaps is more theoretical knowledge that aids in shaping character. But as they appear here, in expositions of poetic parallelism, they both must be taken as sources of moral knowledge that are indispensable for proper behavior. Clearly, this parental teaching forms a lasting source of beauty and adornment for the child (verse 9), just as does a *garland* for the head.

The basic admonition is clear and direct. *If sinners entice you, do not consent* (NRSV; NIV = *do not give in to them*, verse 10). The occasion of the warning is animated by means of a vivid description of the enticement or the "sales appeal" of the evildoer. These persons promise quick, easy money, a tempting attraction now as well as then. In addition, they plead that they are a brotherhood; we share and share alike (verse 14b)! There is camaraderie among thieves! Again, the stylistic technique of parallelism reinforces both the treacherous violence (*lie in wait . . . ; ambush [waylay] . . .*) as well as the enticing appeal.

Verse 15 repeats the initial admonition (verse 10), and functions as an introduction to the real rewards of violence and thievery. Centering on the idea that evil behavior rebounds upon the very head of the perpetrators, the teacher describes clearly their disastrous end (verse 16); they plunge themselves into the abyss of death. To underscore the sheer stupidity of such action, the composer cites a proverbial adage on the unmistakable futility of wickedness. In verse 17, that adage is *how useless to spread a net in full view of all the birds* in the NIV and *for in vain is the net baited while the bird is looking on* in the NRSV. Violence and theft lead only to death and destruction. It is absolute madness and folly to think that one can cheat on the moral system; violence takes away the life of its possessor. Such behavior inevitably sows the seeds of its own destruction.

Wisdom's Prophetic Announcement (1:20-33)

In most places in Proverbs, *wisdom* refers to moral instruction, to some type of perceptive insight into the natural or social order, or to a religious faith in God's orders of creation. But in 1:20-33, as well as in 8:1-36 and 9:1-6, wisdom is personified as a feminine spokesperson for God, pleading for fools and scoffers to give heed to her cries for repentance. From a literary standpoint, the technique of personification is not new to the literature of the Old Testament. It is often used to heighten the colors of nature (Psalms 96:12; 98:7, 8). Inanimate objects spring to life and take on new character when they are transformed into persons. Similar techniques appear in Canaanite mythological texts and in Egyptian wisdom texts. The Egyptian concept of *Maat* (a universal principle of moral order) is personified as a goddess in The Protest of the Eloquent Peasant. Clearly, the Hebrew sages employed highly sophisticated literary expressions in presenting their observations and reflections.

Functioning as a female prophet, Wisdom stations herself at a busy thoroughfare in the city and proceeds to proclaim her message with great force and conviction. First in one place, then in another, she hurries about with a frantic sense of urgency. In a tone that almost begs the fool, she pleads with him to turn and to pay attention to her (verses 22-23). But alas, the fool remains set in his ways, ignores the divine initiative, and plunges himself headlong into disaster. Surprisingly, Lady Wisdom only laughs at the calamity of the fool. But his folly proceeds from only himself. He had his chance to mend his ways. Once the disaster is upon him, it is too late. No help is available at this point; they have to eat the fruit of their ways (verse 31). By contrast, the person who first responds to Wisdom's cry, who repents of his or her folly, is safe, at ease, and well on the way to happiness and well-being (verses 32-33).

The cry of Lady Wisdom to repent (verses 22-23) may sound like similar appeals from the great prophets of the Old Testament, such as Jeremiah and Isaiah. They too issued words of warning, but were ignored for the most part until it was too late and God's judgment was upon the people.

The Benefits of Wisdom (2:1-22)

Describing the attractive benefits of pursuing wisdom, chapter 2 serves as an appropriate introduction to the book of Proverbs. In a noticeable departure from the imperative style, typical in Proverbs 1–9, chapter 2 presents its invitation to taste the fruits of wisdom in a protasis-apodosis form, that is, *if . . . then* (verses 1, 4, 5).

This style clearly shifts the responsibility for achieving wisdom onto the shoulders of human beings. Both knowledge of what is good and the ability to do what is right are clearly within the reach of persons. They have a clear view of the consequences of both wisdom and folly; now they must choose. Even so, the benefits of wisdom are available only to persons who are diligent and serious in their quest. Human effort is required.

A second literary feature heightening the appeal of chapter 2 is parallelism. Through repetition of key ideas (wisdom—understanding, verse 2; fear of the Lord—knowledge of God, verse 5; heart—knowledge, verse 10), much greater clarity and cogency is attained. This style is a monumental tribute to the sage's literary talent.

The central theme of the chapter is that the search for

wisdom/understanding will lead to discovery of the fear of the Lord/knowledge of God. And once we attain this faith, proper moral conduct will follow almost directly. The Hebrew sage believes absolutely in the causal relationship between faith and morality. What a person does is a mirror of who he or she is! From the fear of the Lord comes an understanding of *righteousness and justice and equity* (NRSV; NIV = *What is right and just and fair*), *every good path* (verse 9). The knowledge of God brings deliverance from the temptation to consort with evildoers or with adulterers, precisely because the tragic end and disastrous consequences to such conduct can be foreseen, and it is not an end or a fate to be desired.

Unlike Job 28 or Ecclesiastes 3:11, Proverbs 2 clearly affirms the possibility of human apprehension of God's revelation, that is, of wisdom. Knowledge of God is definitely within a person's reach. God's order of Creation, which dictates human moral conduct, is open to reason, to observation, and to sensory experience. In fact, the failure to use human capabilities in discovering and conforming to God's orders is precisely what is sin to the sage. Willful ignorance is an affront to God.

Peace and security (verses 20-21) come to persons who are upright, while the wicked fall into ruin (*will be cut off from the land*, verse 22).

The Benefits of Faith (3:1-12)

This section consists of six sets of instructions, each validated by motive clauses. Four units are admonitions to refrain from improper behavior (verses 5-9). Although addressing different ethical situations, these six units all recommend strong religious faith as the source for an abundant life.

Verses 1 and 2 urge attention to the speaker's *teachings* and *commandments*. Although in other traditions of biblical thought (namely the Priestly) both of these terms refer to divine law, here they are more inclusive, pointing to many different forms of authoritative instruction. The benefits of these teachings are long years and richness of life. The Hebrew word for *abundant welfare* is *shalom*, which signifies a state of wholeness or peace. The reward of obedience to these instructions is earthly happiness, including abundance, longevity, and peace.

The second set of admonitions (verses 3-4) cautions against losing loyalty and faithfulness to God. These two values must remain constant foundation elements for one's set of ethics. The fruit of this fidelity is personal acceptability to God and others.

The third commandment (verse 5*a*) is an exhortation to rely more on the Lord's grace than on one's own resources. In view of wisdom's general preoccupation with personal morality, industry, and exercise of reason, it seems odd to find a note acquiescing to divine grace (9:12). The tension between divine grace and human effort, however, is a problem throughout the Bible. Human morality is always empowered by divine grace and is motivated by a sincere desire to please the Lord, not by the expectation of reward. The fourth set of instructions (verse 7) underscores the need to avoid egocentric pride.

Verses 9 and 10 suggest that one should make an appropriate offering to God, acknowledging gratitude. This exhortation reminds us of God's laws for the consecration of the first-born (Exodus 13:2). This proper sense of gratitude engenders economic rewards in great measure. But faith is always prior to fortune, as the Job of the prologue clearly demonstrates.

Finally, verses 11 and 12 urge the acceptance of suffering as therapeutic; suffering builds faith and character. Perhaps this advice responds to a fundamental question in Old Testament faith: Why does the innocent person suffer? Clearly, the Job of the discourses (chapters 3–41) complains bitterly that he deserves a better fate (see, for example, Job 9:15-24). Here in Proverbs the answer is that innocent suffering must be understood by way of the analogy of a father disciplining his son in order to make him into a better person. In the sage's view, the Lord chastens human beings in order to help them be better and stronger persons.

Wisdom of God (3:13-20)

Separating the two instruction units in Proverbs 3 are two brief poems extolling the incomparable value of wisdom.

The first poem is a beatitude, reminiscent of Psalm 1 and Matthew 5:3-11. The Hebrew word translated *happy* in the NRSV actually has much deeper meaning, referring to a condition of absolute well-being. Such a state arises from the sense of peace that comes to a person whose faith and life are secure in the knowledge of God, that is, one who has acquired wisdom, one who is *blessed* (NIV). The poem continues by enumerating the many rewards received from wisdom, including intellectual, moral, and economic benefits. The poet alludes to an ancient mythological image, *the tree of life* (Genesis 2:9; 3:22). This is symbolic of strength, abundance, and fruitfulness. Wisdom, like the tree, is an unending source of life and of everything that makes life abundant.

The second poem links God's actions at Creation with wisdom, anticipating Proverbs 8:22-31. Probably, ancient Babylonian and Sumerian mythological creation motifs lay in the poet's mind as he composed this brief piece: the earth being built upon the huge pillars and suspended over primeval waters, the deep as undifferentiated chaos (Genesis 1), and so forth.

The same divine wisdom that was present at Creation, and was watching God at work, is also available to persons on earth, says the sage. Such a knowledge of God comes to those who, by faith, lay hold of wisdom. Just as *the clouds drop down (let drop) the dew* (see verse 20), God calls persons to claim wisdom as a miraculous source of life. The notion of wisdom being present at Creation is developed in much greater detail elsewhere in the book of Proverbs. The purpose of such imagery here and elsewhere is clearly to certify the credibility of wisdom as divine in origin. Since wisdom is divine, it is therefore authoritative and essential.

Moral Instruction (3:21-35)

With verse 21, the instruction unit resumes with an initial exhortation to retain wisdom close at hand, for its benefits are great. The imperative command (verse 21) is introduced by the usual reference to the general audience, *my son* (NIV; NRSV = *my child*). The motive clauses outline the attractive rewards to those persons who possess wisdom, including (1) vibrant spiritual life, (2) physical adornments, (3) steadiness, (4) security, and (5) peace/rest. For the person filled with wisdom, the totality of his or her life rests on firm footing, and he or she need have no cause for alarm when witnessing God's wrath against the wicked ones.

Verses 27-35 describe a person's social obligations, arising from a life informed by wisdom. Among these responsibilities are the following: (1) prompt settlement of debts, (2) fidelity and integrity to one's neighbors, (3) avoiding unnecessary strife, and (4) choosing worthy role-models or heroes.

These social duties engender the favor of the Lord and bring abundant blessings. They reflect the wisdom faith outlined above (verses 21-26). Again, morality and faith belong together.

A Father's Instruction (4:1-27)

The three subdivisions of chapter 4 all begin with the typical introduction, *Listen, my son(s)* (child/children) (verses 1, 10, 20). This opening to the instruction unit in the imperative mood is more than literary formalism: It is a call for attention and respect. Just as he received instructions in wisdom from his parents, so now he instructs his son in the same tradition. The home is the earliest setting for formal instruction, and one's first teachers are his or her parents. At an early age, the young students are introduced to the beauty and benefits of wisdom. In language reminiscent of a loving and devoted wife, wisdom is described as an unending source of pride, protection, and great support. Above all else, wisdom is the treasure worthy of one's full attention and best efforts.

The second section (verses 10-19) contrasts the well-known theme of the two ways or two paths popularized in later Jewish thought (see Psalm 1). Here the path of the wicked (verses 14-17, 19) is described as a dark and treacherous way, in which persons blindly grope along. The appetite of the wicked is voracious and insatiable, requiring a steady gluttony of violence and evil. By contrast, the way of the righteous is a bright and clear way, in which knowledge and clear vision lead one to a long, happy, and fulfilling life. The way of wisdom is a steady way, that avoids the pitfalls of disaster and that shuns the uncertain steps that stumble along aimlessly.

Section three (verses 20-27) is a miscellaneous set of instructions to remain steadfast to moral teaching just as he (the student) had been instructed. The *words* he has been given are words of life that will bring health and abundance. Such *words* must become the object of constant attention and resolute obedience. Apart from counsel to avoid *crooked speech* (NRSV; NIV = *perversity*) which refers to lying or *devious talk* (NRSV; NIV = *corrupt* talk) which refers to malicious gossip, no specific moral instructions are provided. Instead, as in the two preceding sections, the entire unit is a general plea for the student to seek wisdom, to follow the way of righteousness, and to avoid wickedness. The specific do's and don't's await a later chapter.

§ § § § § § §

The Message of Proverbs 1–4

The openly religious nature of these beginning chapters may well surprise the reader who is more accustomed to the practical morality in the sayings of 10:1–22:16. Although absent from chapters 1–4 are references to the great traditions of exodus, election, law, and kingship, Proverbs nonetheless attests to the belief that God established a moral order at Creation, and that life is abundant only with proper regard for this order. The faith of a sage may be different from the faith of a priest or a prophet, but all three groups still affirm the notions of God, of divine revelation, and of human responsibility.

Chapter 2 clearly structures human intellectual knowledge and morality within the realm of religious faith (verses 5-9). Wisdom and understanding, insight and morality (verses 2-3), are not ends in themselves. The goal of reason is not knowledge for the sake of knowledge. The true object of human knowledge and morality is a proper understanding of God and of the orders of Creation. True insight into human existence is impossible apart from faith, and is meaningless without this faith. True insight is insight into how God's world operates and how humankind is intended to fit into this operation.

With this faith, both true understanding and right conduct become clear. Expressed differently, knowledge and morality both lead persons to knowledge of God and follow from the knowledge of God. Perhaps this relationship defies rational comprehension, but ultimately faith, the fear of the Lord, is both the effect and the cause of knowledge and morality.

The second major theme found in Proverbs 1–4 is the delicate balance between human effort and divine grace.

Although this problem may seem more at home in the letters of Paul and in the life of the earliest Christian communities, works versus grace was also a matter of concern to the Old Testament sage.

The sage clearly advocated personal morality, knowledge of act-consequence, and mastery over nature. While these goals were assuredly unattainable apart from faith (3:5), they do seem to be the consequence of human effort. In 4:13-18, wisdom produces life itself! Yet, verses 5-8 suggest that such effort should be secondary and that God supplies the cause of right conduct.

Perhaps the sage feels the dynamic tension between faith and works, and believes that somehow they come together with one nourishing the other. Human righteousness leads to the fear of God and yet, at the same time, proceeds from it. Only in theological analysis are they separable; in actual practice, faith and human effort are synthesized as opposite poles on a magnetic field. They energize each other.

§ § § § § § §

Proverbs 5–9

Introduction to These Chapters

Chapters 5–9 continue the moral teachings begun in chapters 2–4. The principal genre continues to be the instruction, and the style consists of synonymous and synthetic parallelism. In addition to the instruction, these chapters contain a numerical saying (6:16-19), two poems personifying wisdom (8:1-36 and 9:1-6), and an expanded poem detailing the dangers of adultery (chapter 7).

These chapters may be outlined as follows.
  I. Avoiding Temptations from Women (5:1-23)
 II. Instructions Against Wrong Conduct (6:1-35)
III. Instructions to Avoid Adultery (7:1-27)
IV. Wisdom's Second Announcement (8:1-36)
 V. Wisdom and Folly Contrasted (9:1-18)

Avoiding Temptations from Women (5:1-23)

In chapter 5, the warnings against improper sexual conduct (2:16-19) are repeated with even greater urgency due to their disastrous consequences. Verses 1-14 urge young men to avoid succumbing to sexual temptations from *a loose woman* (NRSV; NIV = *adulteress*), and always to maintain a safe distance from their doors. Verses 15-23 encourage marital fidelity based on good reasons, both theological and social.

The introductory section (verses 1-6) addresses the general audience with the typical phrase *my son (child)*. The call to attention (verse 1) receives ample emphasis through synonymous parallelism: *be attentive . . . incline your ear* (NRSV; NIV = *pay attention . . . listen well*). Likewise the motive (verse 2) of the command is stated twice: to *maintain discretion* and to *preserve knowledge* (NIV) or *hold on to prudence* and *guard knowledge* (NRSV). Among the real dangers of consorting with a seductress, the sweetness of her temptation (verse 3) contrasts sharply with the bitterness (verse 4) of the consequences; the smoothness of her inviting words is offset by the sharpness of the fatal results (verse 4). Although parallelism may be somewhat monotonous, the stylistic technique is a truly functional pedagogical tool.

In verses 7-14 the student is admonished to avoid, at all costs, illicit sexual relations. One's procreative powers are essential to the ongoing life of the community and they ought not to be squandered promiscuously. Wrongful indulgence in sexual activities not only diminishes a man's personal honor, his wealth, and his health, but also invites negative judgment within the religious community (verse 14).

In verses 15-23 the same prohibitions are extended to persons who might engage in extramarital sex. Cisterns or wells are well-known images for feminine sexuality in the Old Testament (verse 15). The wife is described in elegant language (verse 19) and as a source of unending joy and delight for her husband. He must limit his sexual activities to her because the eyes of the Lord are watching him and also because his adultery will come back upon him.

Instructions Against Wrong Conduct (6:1-35)

Throughout these nine introductory chapters, persons have been counseled to follow the way of wisdom and to avoid the paths of folly. In chapter 6, these moral norms are made even more specific. Particular behaviors are praised and others are condemned. The opening section (verses 1-5) urges persons to refrain from cosigning for someone else. Although generosity is always considered a virtue in the Old Testament, and the Mosaic law provides for interest-free loans, here the practice of assuming debts for a friend is condemned. In fact the teacher feels so strongly about avoiding such agreements that extreme measures are called for in order to escape the entanglements.

The second section (verses 6-11) urges industriousness and preparedness. As is often the case in proverbial literature of other cultures, the ant is the model of diligence and industriousness. The ant prepares for days when food will not be abundant. Persons should do likewise, else poverty and hunger will befall them. Slothfulness and indolence reap their own rewards.

In the third section (verses 12-15), the sage sketches a behavioral characterization of a wicked person: He lies without conscience, winks his eyes constantly, shuffles his feet, calls undue attention to other persons' faults, and stirs up strife. Such a person truly deserves the calamitous end that most assuredly will befall him. Following the act-consequence order of morality, evil deeds contain the seeds of their own destruction.

The numerical saying (verses 16-19) lists a number of acts that are blatantly offensive to the Lord. The six-seven pattern is a literary expression indicating an infinite number (see Proverbs 30:7-31; Amos 1–2). *Haughty eyes* (verse 17) suggest pride. Lying and murder, scheming, perjury, contentiousness: All are vices that destroy the moral solidarity of the community. No social group can exist for long where these behaviors are tolerated. Trust, honor, respect, and truthfulness are indispensable for an orderly society. Possibly the numerical saying was used in educational settings; the clear, catchy format lends itself well to memory.

The final section (verses 20-35) again urges marital fidelity, as in 5:15-23. Several literary elements add to the beauty of these verses. The extended introduction presents wisdom as a constant shield covering a person, always providing protection. The image of a commandment as a lamp suggests light and clarity of moral vision. Two rhetorical questions (verses 27-28) point to the inevitability of disaster's appearance as a consequence of adultery. No amount of compensation can atone for this act; the offended husband is rife with anger and there is no assuaging him. He will accept no form of appeasement. Likewise society is unforgiving (verse 33).

Adultery occupies more space in Proverbs than any other vice, and perhaps for good reason. Adultery has profound social as well as personal ramifications. It destroys the solidarity of the basic social unit in society: the family. It creates hatred, strife, and mistrust between spouses. It represents a breach of a legal contract. It brings nothing but shame and disgrace to the participants. Although Proverbs imposes the initial responsibility on the female as the initiator, both parties must pay the consequences. We must remember also that early Israelite society was very much male-oriented, and the author of these instructions was probably a male.

Instructions to Avoid Adultery (7:1-27)

Chapter 7 continues the theme of avoiding adultery, begun in 6:20. The chapter may be divided clearly into three sections: introduction (including summons and purpose) (verses 1-5), poetic narrative (verses 6-23), and concluding admonitions (verses 24-27). Like most instructions, chapter 7 identifies the audience with the customary formula *my son (child)*. The student-hearers are urged to pay close attention to these lessons, to make them a part of their daily lives, and to remember them carefully. The images conveyed by words such as *apple of your eye, fingers,* and *tablet of your heart* add to the fundamental importance of these instructions, as well as to the aesthetic quality.

Rather than the typical set of individual imperative sayings usually found in the instruction units, chapter 7 is an extended poetical narrative describing the seduction of a young and foolish boy. This event is told and evaluated through the eyes of a watchful sage. The entire episode occurs just at twilight, lending it a sinister air. The woman exudes passion and desire as she entices the young and foolish lad with food (portions remaining from her sacrificial offerings earlier), with fine decorations at home, and with fragrant scents. She assures him that they are safe, because her husband is away on a trip and carried along a huge sum of money. The temptation is too strong for the lad to withstand and so he follows her, follows her to certain death.

The unit concludes (verses 24-27) with a final word of warning from the sage to avoid the temptations of illicit sexual relations. The adulteress's offer carries, in reality, too high a price. It will cost him his life: both his physical life, should her husband return unexpectedly, and his spiritual life, since he has violated one of God's moral orders. The strength to resist these sexual temptations lies in the words or commandments of the teacher, that is, his wisdom (verse 4).

Wisdom's Second Announcement (8:1-36)

This is an uplifting, inspiring poem describing Wisdom's appeal and promise. Here Wisdom is depicted as a feminine prophet, summoning all persons to partake of her knowledge, for she brings life and health and understanding. The adulteress brought death, suffering, and despair. The sharp contrast between the two could not be more pronounced or more intentional.

Chapter 8 consists of four sections: (1) introduction (verses 1-11), (2) the earthly benefits of Wisdom (verses 12-21), (3) the divine sanction of Wisdom (verses 22-31), and (4) final summons and motive (verses 32-36). The unit begins with a third-person address describing Wisdom's intense search for hearers. The rhetorical question (verse 1) affirms Wisdom's initiative; she makes the first move toward persons. The Lady Wisdom herself speaks. And she chooses a public place where large crowds gather: at the gate to the town. How different is her setting from the darkened streets of the adulteress in chapter 7!

The second section (verses 12-21) continues the first-person style, and cites the impressive accomplishments and rewards that Wisdom has attained on earth. In her, persons discover the essential connection between faith and morality (verse 13). Wisdom has also proven helpful to kings, princes, and rulers, as well as to persons of non-royal estates. Wealth beyond all measure springs from her well, but more important, righteousness and justice are her fruits.

But Wisdom has also another sanction. She was created by God at the very beginning of her work, and was a watchful onlooker as God laid out the orders of the universe. She was God's delight! She played in the presence of God as God created the world (verses 22-31). That Wisdom was watching and rejoicing as God fashioned the world has led to much speculation as to exactly what was the intended relationship between God and Wisdom. Although verse 30 is obscure, the term is translated as *master worker* in the NRSV or as *craftsman* in the NIV. Was *Wisdom* a kind of pre-existent being, separate from God? Or was Wisdom thought to be the *intellectual expression* of a divine will, a form of revelation available to persons on earth? Answers to these questions are made more difficult by grammatical problems and by often obscure words in the Hebrew text. Clearly the editor intended that Wisdom be closely associated to God and be as old as Creation itself.

Since, metaphorically speaking, Wisdom was present at Creation, she certainly must understand the orders of the world. The strongly mythological imagery in verses 27-29 suggests a primeval cosmology similar to that used by the Priestly writer and found in Genesis 1–2. Also, the notion of a pre-existent form of divine revelation stands behind the New Testament concept of *logos* in John 1:1-3. Wisdom discloses God's orders and enables persons both to know and to do that which is right. More is said on this subject in the section at the close of this chapter.

The conclusion (verses 32-34) contains two imperatives on obtaining wisdom (verse 33), and a final observation stating the ultimate consequences of Wisdom (verses 35-36). The word *happy* (NRSV) actually refers to a state of peace and contentment that arises from faith and knowledge, and is better translated *blessed* (NIV). The reference to gates and doors ties the conclusion to the introduction.

Wisdom and Folly Contrasted (9:1-18)

Chapter 9 certainly must have had a very interesting and complicated literary history, for incongruities among its three sections make interpretation difficult. Apparently the editor sets up a contrast between Wisdom's invitation to her banquet in verses 1-6, and Folly's enticement in verses 13-18.

The opening section presents Wisdom's invitation to attend a special banquet in her house (verses 1-6). Elaborate preparations have been made: special meat, aromatic wine, careful place-settings. Her house, erected upon (or around) seven columns, suggests wealth and opulence. The invitation is extended particularly to those persons who are young, inexperienced, and who lack proper knowledge. Obviously they stand to profit the most from such a meal. The heralds of Wisdom's invitation are her servants who are sent openly into public places where the largest audiences are to be found. The invitation is simple and straightforward: Come, eat, and live!

By contrast, Folly's invitation is almost repulsive. Her shameless and wanton demeanor are symptomatic of her inner wretchedness. She lures the unsuspecting by the enticement of sex. She cites an old adage to support her appeal to enjoy "forbidden foods": *Stolen water is sweet . . .* (verse 17). Both Wisdom and Folly appeal to the same audience, the young and inexperienced. But the meals they serve and the effects are clearly different.

The center section (verses 7-12) is a collection of different sayings, contrasting the scoffer and the wise man. Hidden among these sayings is a declaration that serves as the theological thesis for the entire book, as expressed in verse 10: *The fear of the LORD is the beginning of wisdom, and the knowledge of the Holy One is insight (understanding)*. Concluding this section is a saying that introduces a new concept on individual responsibility (verse 12). The choice of whether to be wise or to be a scoffer is up to each person, and for that choice he or she is solely responsible. Possibly this saying is the key to interpreting the chapter as a whole. Two invitations come to a person, to attend banquets hosted by Wisdom and Folly. One may attend either banquet. And it is up to each individual to decide whose invitation to accept. Through the teachings of the sages, persons become sufficiently knowledgeable to know whose "house" to visit.

§ § § § § § §

The Message of Proverbs 5–9

Proverbs 5–9 contains several major themes that are of great significance in the religious life of ancient Israel. The sages made serious attempts to define specific behavior that surely led to disaster: fornication, adultery, unwise debt assumption, indolence and lack of advanced planning and preparation, lying, stirring up dissension, and so forth. These chapters also introduce the important notion of individual responsibility (9:12). Proverbs 6:20-35 contrasts the life-giving light of wisdom with the fateful end of folly. These themes reinforce the notion that, for the sage, religious belief and proper moral conduct are inseparable.

Another theme emerging from these chapters is the relationship between Wisdom and Creation. In chapter 8 Wisdom describes herself as being present when God was creating the world (8:22-23). Then Wisdom turned and became available to humans, as a source of ultimate understanding, giving persons insight into the mysteries of God.

§ § § § § § §

PART THREE

Proverbs 10–14

Introduction to These Chapters

Chapter 10 begins a new section of Proverbs, distinct
from chapters 1–9. It begins with a new superscription in
verse 1. Also, there is a change in style from extended
poems, instructions, and shorter poems, to two-line
sayings characterized by parallelism. For more
background information on Proverbs 10:1–22:16, see the
Introduction to Proverbs on pages 14-20.

The Proverbs of Solomon, I (10:1-32)

Verse 1: Antithetical parallelism intensifies the contrast
between the joy of wisdom and the sorrow of folly, as
exhibited in a child's behavior. Moral conduct in a child
is always a source of pride or shame to the parents. See
also 15:20; 17:21, 25.

Verse 2: This saying contrasts the life-giving benefits of
wisdom with the death-bringing consequences of folly.
Treasures gained by wickedness are often short-lived and
illusory (see 10:22). The parallelism is antithetical.

Verse 3: Divine support for righteous persons,
particularly economic benefits, ensures their earthly
well-being. Divine retribution, likewise, provides
sufficient judgment against the evildoer (see 15:29). The
parallelism is antithetical.

Verse 4: Hard work and industriousness, practiced by
the sages, are always positive moral virtues. Such
behavior is usually economically productive, and the

sages represent responsible stewardship of personal resources (see 12:11, 24). The parallelism in this saying is antithetical.

Verse 5: The point of this saying is similar to that of verse 4. Here, however, the additional element of proper timing suggests insight into the annual cycles of nature. The parallelism is antithetical.

Verse 6: The righteous person's good behavior brings blessings and favor; the evildoer's mouth harbors suffering and violence. The parallelism is antithetical.

Verse 7: In addition to the temporal blessings of righteousness mentioned in verse 6, another reward is the lasting impression of love and respect that moral conduct forms in the memory of other persons. By contrast, popular recollection of the wicked person quickly disappears. The proverb uses antithetical parallelism.

Verse 8: Wise persons realize they have much to learn; fools think they have nothing to learn. See also 12:1; 13:1. The parallelism is antithetical.

Verse 9: Antithetical parallelism conveys the message that proper moral conduct brings a life free from worry.

Verse 10: Honesty is always preferable to deception. A winking eye often suggests sly action.

Verse 11: See also 10:6; 11:6; 14:27; 16:22. The parallelism is antithetical.

Verse 12: The proverb stresses the value of love in relationships, using antithetical parallelism.

Verse 13: For the person of understanding, wisdom is a sufficient guide. But stronger measures are necessary to correct an obstinate fool.

Verse 14: Lay up (NRSV; NIV = *store up*) is more properly translated *conceal*. The wise carefully choose their words while fools talk themselves into trouble. See also 15:2.

Verse 15: See also 18:11. The proverb uses antithetical parallelism.

Verse 16: See also 11:6, 8, 19. The parallelism is antithetical.

Verse 17: This saying notes the advantages of accepting positive criticism. See also 12:1.

Verse 18: Synthetical parallelism is used to convey the idea that deception and gossip are both morally wrong.

Verse 19: See also 15:2, 4.

Verse 20: Silver is a precious metal. A person's tongue expresses the ideas of his or her mind.

Verse 21: The term *feed* (NRSV; NIV = *nourish*) refers either to how a wise person produces economic benefits, or to how a wise person nourishes (spiritually) all who listen. In either case, a fool starves.

Verse 22: True prosperity comes from the Lord.

Verses 23-25: These proverbs all use antithetical parallelism.

Verse 26: The parallelism between lazy persons and bitter vinegar (or irritating smoke) is synthetical.

Verses 27-32: These proverbs all use antithetical parallelism.

The Proverbs of Solomon, II (11:1-31)

The proverbs contained in this chapter are virtually all of the antithetical type.

Verse 1: God's concern for a system of accurate weight and measurement signals a special concern to protect the interests and needs of the poor.

Verse 2: Conceit and arrogance produce contempt; humility earns respect.

Verse 3: This saying illustrates the direct connection the sages saw between acts and consequences.

Verse 4: Usually, the expression *day of wrath* refers to a national day of judgment when divine punishment comes forth (see Zephaniah 1:15-18). Here the phrase refers to the day of one's death.

Verse 5: Proper moral conduct brings peace and safety; wickedness plunges persons into a deep abyss.

Verse 6: See also 11:3, 5. These sayings exhibit the natural operations of divine retribution.

Verse 7: Here the parallelism is synonymous. This saying dispels any hope the wicked have for lasting influence on others. See also 10:28.

Verse 8: See 10:16; 11:5-6.

Verse 9: See 10:31-32.

Verse 10: Morality is not a totally private affair; moral behavior has important civic ramifications.

Verse 11: See also 11:10. Here, wicked persons bring destruction to their city. Blessings come to the city from the good deeds of righteous persons.

Verse 12: See also 10:19.

Verse 13: Gossip always fractures human relationships; silence and trustworthiness engender peace. See also 11:9; 20:19.

Verse 14: Properly trained leadership is necessary to lead a nation successfully. This saying could be a reference to Israel's need for a king.

Verse 15: This saying seems to contradict the Mosaic laws regarding generosity and help for one's neighbor.

Verse 16: This saying contrasts the lasting value of honor gained by a virtuous woman with the temporal, economic wealth amassed by a man of violence.

Verse 17: See also 11:5-6.

Verses 18-19: See also 10:16-17.

Verse 20: This saying connects divine attitude with personal morality. Whereas in the cultic laws in Leviticus, ritual perfection is demanded by the Lord, here moral perfection is God's desire.

Verse 21: See also 11:5-6.

Verse 22: This comparative saying points to two incongruities: a priceless metal in a pig's nose and a beautiful woman with bad morals. These situations represent perversions of the moral order.

Verse 23: See also 10:24.

Verse 24: This saying is directed toward help for the needy.

Verses 25-26: See also 11:24.

Verse 27: See 11:5-6.

Verse 28: From the domain of nature, the sage contrasts the fruitful conduct of a righteous person with the barrenness that comes to the wicked.

Verse 29: Trouble may refer either to disruption in family relationships or to economic deprivation.

Verses 30-31: See also 10:16-17; 11:19, 28.

The Proverbs of Solomon, III (12:1-28)

Unless otherwise indicated, the proverbs in this section use antithetical parallelism.

Verse 1: An important indication of real knowledge is the willingness to accept correction and learn from mistakes.

Verse 2: This saying is a clear affirmation of divine retribution (see also 11:20).

Verse 3: See also 10:30; 11:4-5. The root established by righteousness refers to a source of strength and nourishment.

Verse 4: A wife of good intellect and moral character is an asset to her husband; stupidity and folly in a wife are a fatal disease.

Verse 5: Righteous persons are concerned to deal justly with others; evildoers are a threat to society.

Verse 6: See 1:8-19; 11:19.

Verse 7: See 10:25; 11:5; 12:3.

Verse 8: This saying is a positive comment on public recognition of superior knowledge. Faith and morality are part of this knowledge.

Verse 9: The parallelism is synonymous, stressing the value of personal integrity.

Verse 10: This saying may reflect an agricultural or pastoral setting.

Verse 11: See also 10:5. This saying is one of many

similar proverbs stressing diligence and industry. Note particularly the non-religious, utilitarian character of this proverb.

Verse 12: Although the Hebrew of this verse is difficult to translate, it seems to contrast the stability of the righteous with the precariousness of the wicked.

Verse 13: See also 10:31-32; 11:5. The *sinful talk* (NIV) or *transgression of the lips* of the evil refer to slander, lies, or idle gossip.

Verse 14: The act-consequence sequence returns good for good. See also 11:8. Synonymous parallelism is used.

Verse 15: See also 3:7; 12:1.

Verse 16: The point of this saying is that persons should remain calm in the face of personal insults.

Verse 17: This saying may have had its setting in the legal community. It attests to the merits of truthfulness over perjury.

Verse 18: Proper speech brings peace and harmony.

Verse 19: The enduring effects of truthfulness are contrasted with the transience of falsehood.

Verse 20: A person's inner motives are very important in doing what is righteous.

Verse 21: See also 11:31; 12:12.

Verse 22: Here lying is presented as the subject of divine condemnation.

Verse 23: See also 10:14, 19. Silence is golden.

Verse 24: This astute observation on business life recognizes that the person who works hard and perseveres will soon become the employer of the fool.

Verse 25: This saying records a true insight into human psychology: Worry depresses persons, but words of cheer make persons happy.

Verse 26: See 12:6, 12.

Verse 27: The Hebrew of this verse is difficult. As translated in the NIV and NRSV, the saying indicates the rewards of diligence and the paltry gains of sloth.

Verse 28: See 11:30; 12:6.

The Proverbs of Solomon, IV (13:1-25)

Almost all the proverbs in this chapter are of the antithetical type.

Verse 1: See also 12:1.

Verse 2: See 12:14.

Verse 3: Careful speech is preferable to constant chatter; see also 10:19.

Verse 4: The rewards of hard work and laziness are contrasted.

Verse 5: See also 12:22. Proper moral conduct is attractive to a righteous person; a wicked person revels in the ignorance of violence.

Verse 6: See also 12:12, 26.

Verse 7: The saying indicates that economic well-being is not always what it may seem; true wealth is a matter of character.

Verse 9: This is the first saying in Proverbs that uses the imagery of light or a lamp.

Verse 10: See 12:1; 13:1.

Verse 11: Business and finance provide ample material for the work of the sage. Here, a cautious approach to the accumulation of wealth is preferred to quick, risky speculation.

Verse 12: The anxiety caused by continued frustration is contrasted with the joy that comes from achievements.

Verse 13: The parallelism between *word* and *commandment* (NRSV; NIV = *instruction* and *command*) probably refers to the divine Word (that is, wisdom, or *torah*).

Verse 14: The parallelism is synthetic. See also 11:30; 12:6, 8.

Verse 15: See also 12:8.

Verse 16: See also 12:23.

Verse 17: This saying points to the awesome power of a messenger to bring peace.

Verse 18: See 12:1; 13:1.

Verse 19: This saying begins with a general observation

about human nature: One usually rejoices when a goal has been attained. Then the principle is applied in reverse to the fool.

Verse 20: Righteousness and foolishness are both contagious.

Verse 21: Divine retribution is the moral order of society.

Verse 22: This saying is an observation about family life, rather than an instruction.

Verse 23: Again, this saying is an observation rather than an instruction. Injustice occurs when one is deprived of the benefits of one's labor by social or economic evil.

Verse 24: Failure to correct the misdeeds of one's children is a sign of weakness, not of love.

Verse 25: See also 10:3.

The Proverbs of Solomon, V (14:1-35)

Most of the proverbs in this chapter are antithetical.

Verse 1: This saying celebrates the role of women in a household; they actually dictate its welfare.

Verse 2: Morality is a proper affirmation of faith.

Verse 3: See also 10:19; 12:13; 13:3.

Verse 4: The Hebrew text is obscure. Following the NRSV, the saying attests to the importance of the ox in providing food.

Verse 5: See 12:17. Perjury is unacceptable to a righteous person.

Verse 6: Laziness robs persons both of material well-being and of wisdom.

Verse 7: See 13:20.

Verse 8: The decision about which path to follow is easy for the righteous person and difficult for the fool.

Verse 9: Wickedness is an offense to God.

Verse 10: This saying is not formal instruction; it is an introspective look into the privacy of one's heart. No one can see inside there, unless allowed.

Verse 11: See also 12:28; 13:6, 9.

Verse 12: See also 16:25.

Verse 13: The pessimism reflected here seems out of place in the book of Proverbs; it would be more at home in Ecclesiastes. The irony of laughter is that one can be sad yet laughing at the same time. Sometimes joy contains elements of grief.

Verse 14: See 11:30; 12:14.

Verse 15: One consequence of ignorance is a state of being too trustful.

Verse 16: See also 13:16.

Verse 17: The point of the saying is that patience is preferable to haste.

Verse 18: An intelligent person can achieve true understanding, while the simple-minded person turns to folly.

Verse 19: Eventually, goodness triumphs over evil. The proverb uses synonymous parallelism.

Verse 20: This observation records an unfortunate social situation; wealth brings popularity while poverty searches for friends.

Verse 21: This saying shows concern for the poor and needy of society.

Verse 22: A rhetorical question introduces this reflection. No one can be truly happy and desire evil at the same time.

Verse 23: Hard work yields success; idle chatter yields wind.

Verse 24: A crown is a symbol of authority and power; such is the wisdom of the wise person.

Verse 25: See also 12:17, 22; 14:5.

Verse 26: Synthetic parallelism is used here.

Verse 27: Faith is a source of life.

Verse 28: Synonymous parallelism is used to state that reciprocal needs exist between a king and his people.

Verse 29: See also 14:17.

Verse 30: Unbridled passion often causes personal and social chaos.

Verse 31: In the Old Testament, considerable care is taken to protect the rights of the poor and to provide for their needs. But the *poor* and the *needy* are two separate groups and are not to be confused.

Verse 32: See 12:7, 28.

Verse 33: To strengthen the parallelism and clarify an obscure Hebrew text, the Greek translation adds *not* in the second line. Now the saying contrasts the presence of understanding in a wise person and its absence in a fool.

Verse 34: The saying refers to Israel's faith in God and disdain for apostasy.

Verse 35: A prudent and trustworthy servant always engenders the king's favor.

§ § § § § § §

The Message of Proverbs 10–14

Few new theological insights emerge in this section. Rather, righteousness is defined by many new examples, and the way of folly receives judgment. Specific virtues—honesty in court, compassion for the poor, judicious speech, hard work, patience—characterize the righteous person. The rewards of this proper conduct are divine favor, longevity, community esteem, prosperity, and peace of mind. This proper morality arises from faith (the fear of the Lord).

This connection between creed and conduct is reciprocal—one cannot function effectively without the other. Undergirding this effort to instill morality, the sages affirm over and over again the principle of divine retribution—the Lord rewards the righteous and punishes the wicked, here on earth. Divine judgment (or reward) is not postponed.

§ § § § § § §

Proverbs 15–18

Introduction to These Chapters

These chapters continue the collection of short, one-line sayings that began in chapter 10. All the proverbs in this section are attributed to Solomon.

The Proverbs of Solomon, VI (15:1-33)

Most of the proverbs in this chapter are of the antithetical type.

Verse 1: This observation states that a calm, peaceful response assuages anger, whereas a sharp retort merely inflames a hostile situation.

Verse 2: See 10:11, 20; 14:33.

Verse 3: Here the parallelism is synthetic; the message is that God can reward or punish persons appropriately, knowing the deeds of all those on earth.

Verse 4: This saying is similar to that in verse 1.

Verse 5: See also 12:1; 13:1.

Verse 6: This message is similar to that of 13:21; 14:11, 14.

Verse 7: See also 15:2.

Verse 8: Acts of religious devotion cannot be separated from proper morality; see Amos 5:21-24; Micah 6:8.

Verse 9: See also 12:22; 14:9.

Verse 10: Synonymous parallelism conveys the message that the consequence of ignoring wise instruction and committing wickedness is death.

Verse 11: Here the parallelism is synthetical; see 15:3.

Verse 12: Only fools refuse to heed advice or to accept correction.

Verse 13: Inward attitude affects outward behavior, so the joys of a wise heart are clearly visible.

Verse 14: The appetites of the wise and the foolish are very different; one hungers for knowledge and the other is satisfied with folly.

Verse 16: This comparative saying contrasts the virtue of faith with folly. True wealth does not consist solely of material prosperity.

Verse 17: Here the parallelism is comparative.

Verse 18: See also 14:17; 15:1.

Verse 19: Many dangerous obstacles line the road traveled by the sluggard; the wise person travels easily on an open thoroughfare.

Verse 20: See also 10:1.

Verse 21: Only a person without understanding finds joy in ignorance; a wise person enjoys the blessings of knowledge and morality.

Verse 22: This observation applies equally well to an individual who heeds instruction and to a nation governed by a wise ruler.

Verse 23: A favorite theme in Proverbs is proper speech. Synonymous parallelism conveys the message that proper timing is important as well.

Verse 24: Since heaven, in the Old Testament, is considered to be the abode of God (not of deceased souls), the contrast is between the joyous life of persons on earth and the doleful existence in Sheol after death. The parallelism is synthetic.

Verse 25: This saying would be more appropriate to the classical prophets such as Amos, Jeremiah, or Isaiah. Persons of power and wealth who abuse the poor and the weak are the objects of divine wrath.

Verse 26: See also 11:20; 15:9.

Verse 27: Wealth that is acquired by unjust means

brings no joy; however, honesty always leads to peace and joy.

Verse 28: See also 10:19; 13:3; 15:2.

Verse 29: See 14:9; 15:8.

Verse 30: To preserve proper parallelism, the *light of the eyes* (NRSV; NIV = *a cheerful look*) refers to the exhilaration that comes from receiving good news.

Verse 31: See 15:5.

Verse 32: See 13:1; 15:31.

Verse 33: See 1:7; 9:10; 14:27.

The Proverbs of Solomon, VII (16:1-33)

Verse 1: This is the first in a series of sayings that all contain the name of the Lord (except verse 8). See also 16:9.

Verse 2: Human pretensions do not escape divine scrutiny.

Verse 3: Righteous conduct arises from a true sense of faith.

Verse 4: This saying is a clear affirmation of divine determinism. The parallelism is synonymous.

Verse 5: Divine judgment is absolutely certain for the sinner. See also 11:20-21.

Verse 6: This saying, which uses synthetic parallelism, conveys a message similar to that of Micah 6:1-8.

Verse 7: This saying points to a high moral standard: Righteousness and sincere faith calm even the most volatile enemies.

Verse 8: *Righteousness* here replaces the fear of the Lord (see 15:16). Comparative parallelism conveys the message that morality and faith are opposite sides of the same coin.

Verse 9: Ultimately, as well as right now, a person's destiny belongs in the hands of God.

Verse 10: In general, the sages appear to approve of monarchy, particularly because it brings necessary social order. Thus, the words of a wise ruler deserve attention.

Verse 11: Synonymous parallelism is used; the saying makes the point that matters of economic justice such as proper weights and measurements are established by God. Therefore, they are not arbitrary, even for the king.

Verse 12: The king is not above God's law, but is subject to it, as is everyone else.

Verse 13: Synonymous parallelism is used.

Verse 14: Synthetic parallelism is used.

Verse 15: Synonymous parallelism conveys the idea that a royal blessing can bestow life itself.

Verses 16-18: These sayings use synonymous parallelism.

Verse 19: See also 15:16-17; the parallelism here is comparative.

Verse 20: The parallelism is synonymous; see also 13:13; 15:31; Psalm 1.

Verse 21: Wise words are convincing words. The saying uses synthetical parallelism.

Verse 22: See also 10:11; 11:30.

Verse 23: The subject is the convincing logic of the wise; the parallelism is synthetical.

Verse 24: Synthetic parallelism is used; words of wisdom produce positive effects both inwardly and outwardly.

Verse 25: See also 14:12.

Verse 26: This saying is probably a sarcastic observation on the earthy motivations of much human effort and toil.

Verses 27-28: Wicked words destroy life and cause severe social disruption.

Verse 29: See 1:8-19.

Verse 30: Synonymous parallelism is used; the subject is certain forms of body language that signify devious intent.

Verse 31: *Gray hair* from old age is a sign of divine blessing.

Verse 32: The parallelism is synonymous; see 14:17.

Verse 33: This saying repeats the thought of verse 1.

The Proverbs of Solomon, VIII (17:1-28)

Verse 1: See also 15:16-17.

Verse 2: This observation notes the fair and generous opportunities given to slaves in early Israel.

Verse 3: In a way similar to the process for refining precious metals, God discovers and judges true character in a person's heart.

Verse 4: Synonymous parallelism is used. This saying registers an astute observation on social relationships: Like attracts like.

Verse 5: The saying uses synthetic parallelism; see also 14:31.

Verse 6: This saying celebrates the strength of family ties, using synthetical parallelism.

Verse 7: Synthetical parallelism is used; see also 11:22.

Verse 8: This saying is a sarcastic comment on the practice of bribery.

Verse 9: Antithetical parallelism is used.

Verse 10: This saying uses synthetic parallelism.

Verse 11: The most likely interpretation of *rebellion* is a revolt against divine authority. If so, the second line affirms divine retribution.

Verse 12: Synthetical parallelism conveys the message that folly is exceedingly dangerous.

Verse 13: Failure to express proper gratitude results in divine punishment.

Verse 14: This exhortation warns that angry relationships that linger only intensify.

Verse 15: Judicial unfairness was particularly disturbing to the sage. See also 24:24.

Verse 16: In style, this saying is a rhetorical question; see also 16:22.

Verse 17: Synonymous parallelism is used; the subject is the nature of true friendship.

Verse 18: This saying describes the dangers involved in cosigning for a friend.

Verse 19: Synonymous parallelism is used.

Verse 20: See also 14:11; the subject is divine retribution.

Verse 21: Synonymous parallelism is used; see also 10:1.

Verse 22: See also 15:13; 16:21.

Verse 23: Bribery is a repulsive form of social injustice.

Verse 24: Again, the wise and foolish are contrasted, using antithetical parallelism.

Verse 25: See also 10:1; verse 21.

Verse 26: Judicial injustice offends God and undermines the moral fabric of society.

Verse 27: Careful speech and a calm temperament characterize the wise person.

Verse 28: Silence is golden, even for the fool.

The Proverbs of Solomon, IX (18:1-24)

Verse 2: This saying uses synthetical parallelism.

Verse 3: The social consequences of folly add to its undesirable nature.

Verse 4: Language is a matter of great importance, and wisdom is a constant source of blessing and security.

Verse 5: The subject is fairness in the judicial system.

Verses 6-7: See also 15:2, 4; synonymous parallelism is used.

Verse 8: The *words of a whisperer* (NRSV) probably refer to those of a slanderer or an idle *gossip* (NIV).

Verse 9: See also 12:11, 24, 27.

Verse 10: In the ancient Near East, names conveyed the essence of someone or something.

Verse 11: This saying registers the observation that wealth has its benefits. The tone is neutral rather than passing judgment on the wealthy.

Verse 12: See also 16:18.

Verse 13: This is a conditional saying; the subject is hasty answers given without due thought.

Verse 14: See also 15:13; 17:22.

Verse 15: See 14:33. The parallelism is synonymous.

Verse 16: Patronage and friendship are to be distinguished from bribery.

Verse 17: This saying comes from the legal tradition. Cross-examination often exposes matters in a different light, and opinions can be changed.

Verse 18: Since God was believed to control the sacred lots, using them enabled God's will to prevail where choices needed to be made.

Verses 20-22: See also 12:14.

Verse 23: The arrogance of the wealthy is contrasted with the humility of the poor.

Verse 24: This is a comment on the nature of friendship; some interpersonal relationships are deeper and more permanent than others.

§ § § § § § §

The Message of Proverbs 15–18

In chapter 16, God's name appears in eight of the first nine sayings. Three of these eight sayings (verses 1, 4, and 9) affirm the notion of divine determinism (that is, the idea that earthly events occur according to God's will, for some higher purpose). See especially verse 4*a*.

Later in the same chapter, verse 33 states that even the sacred lots fall at the Lord's will. Collectively, these four sayings argue for more than divine foreknowledge; they insist that there is a causal relationship between events on earth and God's will. Human existence falls under divine control. Human beings are not the makers of history, but history's recipients.

Clearly, divine determinism eliminates the reality of human freedom (see Deuteronomy 30:15; Proverbs 12:11). Human guilt is also called into question. That is, how can God hold persons responsible unless they have the freedom and ability to do something other than what they did? Yet, according to Proverbs 16, we have no real part to play in the events that befall us. This is indeed a paradox! Both divine determinism and human freedom can be documented in the Old Testament.

§ § § § § § §

PART FIVE Proverbs 19:1–22:16

Introduction to These Chapters

These chapters continue the sayings under the heading *Proverbs of Solomon* (see 10:1).

The Proverbs of Solomon, X (19:1-29)

Verse 1: This comparative-style saying advocates maintaining one's personal honor at the expense of gaining wealth.

Verse 2: Forethought is preferable to a hasty act that lacks purpose; the parallelism is synthetical.

Verse 3: Evil persons refuse to accept their own guilt.

Verse 4: See also verse 7; 14:20.

Verse 5: Synonymous parallelism is used; the subject is perjury.

Verse 6: Synonymous parallelism is used; this saying contrasts with verse 4.

Verse 7: This saying contains a third line, a form that is unusual in this section of Proverbs. See verse 4.

Verse 8: This saying uses synonymous parallelism.

Verse 9: See also verse 5.

Verse 10: This saying describes two incongruous social situations.

Verse 11: Synonymous parallelism conveys the message that a slow temper and a willingness to forgive are two prudent virtues.

Verse 12: Lions were common animals in Palestine during biblical times.

Verse 13: The sage finds a foolish son and a nagging wife particularly distressing in view of the contributions they could make to the family's welfare.

Verse 14: The *prudent* wife is here contrasted to the nagging wife of the previous saying.

Verse 15: Synonymous parallelism is used; see also 20:13.

Verse 16: See also 13:13.

Verse 17: Synonymous parallelism is used; the subject is compassion for the poor.

Verse 18: This saying instructs parents in how to exercise "hard love" toward their children.

Verse 19: This saying is difficult to translate due to a corrupt Hebrew text. As translated in the NIV and NRSV, the saying warns against the dangers of unchecked anger and the futility of trying to help a hot-tempered person.

Verse 20: This saying urges persons to heed proper instruction in order to achieve happiness.

Verse 21: See also 16:1, 9.

Verse 22: Although the Hebrew is difficult to translate, the general sense seems to be that a trustworthy friend who is poor is preferable to a dishonest friend who is rich.

Verse 23: The path of faith leads to an abundant and satisfying life.

Verse 24: See also 26:15.

Verse 25: Two methods of instruction are needed for two different personalities: strong force for reluctant learners and simple correction for persons of wisdom.

Verse 26: See also Exodus 20:12.

Verse 27: See also 8:33.

Verse 28: Synonymous parallelism is used; the subject is the legal or social harm that can be caused by an evil tongue.

Verse 29: Strong punishments come to wicked persons, according to this saying.

The Proverbs of Solomon, XI (20:1-30)

Verse 1: The effects produced by intoxicants are personified as the drinks themselves.

Verse 2: Angering a king may be hazardous; the saying uses synonymous parallelism.

Verse 3: See also 17:14.

Verse 4: See also 12:11; the parallelism is synonymous.

Verse 5: Understanding brings power to the wise.

Verse 6: The second line is a rhetorical question; the message is that persons of integrity are hard to find.

Verse 7: A righteous father leaves a legacy of integrity and blessedness to his children.

Verse 8: A king is obligated to separate truth from falsehood.

Verse 9: This saying indirectly proposes the notion of universal sinfulness: All persons sin and fall short of God's glory.

Verse 10: See 11:1; 16:11.

Verse 11: Even in children, true character expresses itself in conduct.

Verse 12: Since human beings are creations of God, we are obligated to use our senses wisely.

Verse 13: See also 12:11; 19:15.

Verse 14: This kind of behavior is typical in oriental bazaars, even today.

Verse 15: See also 15:2.

Verse 16: Anyone who is foolish enough to guarantee another's debts should be held to the promise.

Verse 17: Wealth obtained through dishonesty may be pleasant at first, but will later turn sour.

Verse 18: Careful thought and sound advice should precede all ventures of state, especially war.

Verse 19: The style is negative instruction; see also 11:13.

Verse 20: Cursing one's parents violates a commandment of God (see Exodus 21:17).

Verse 21: Inheritance (NIV; NRSV = *estate*) may be taken

broadly to mean wealth accumulated from one's own efforts as well as wealth received from parents. Quick riches may be short-lived.

Verse 22: See also 24:24; the style is negative instruction.

Verse 23: Economic justice is a matter of importance to God as well as to the business community.

Verse 24: The style is rhetorical question; see also 16:1-9.

Verse 25: Impulsive religious promises should be avoided.

Verse 26: A king must separate evildoers from the righteous in order to preserve order in his kingdom.

Verse 27: The divine spirit, which enlivens all persons, serves as an inner light, mirroring their true character.

Verse 28: Synonymous parallelism is used; see also 16:10.

Verse 29: A sense of pride in certain physical attributes is appropriate.

Verse 30: Stern punishment can have a therapeutic value.

The Proverbs of Solomon, XII (21:1-31)

Verse 1: As an engineer cuts irrigation channels where he chooses, so God directs the work of kings.

Verse 2: Self-justification and divine justification are entirely different matters.

Verse 3: Morality takes precedence over religious sacrifice in satisfying one's obligation to the Lord.

Verse 4: The eye and the heart were thought to be the two principal sources of knowledge—sensory knowledge and spiritual knowledge.

Verse 5: Usually the diligent are contrasted with the lazy; here, however, they are contrasted with hasty, unthinking persons who aspire to quick riches.

Verse 6: Wealth obtained by dishonest means dissipates quickly.

Verse 7: Synonymous parallelism conveys the message that violence begets violence.

Verse 8: This saying contrasts the crooked way of the evildoer with the straight path of the righteous person.

Verse 9: The parallelism is comparative; see 18:22.

Verse 10: Synonymous parallelism is used.

Verse 11: Different persons require different teaching methods; see also 19:25.

Verse 12: This saying is difficult to interpret; perhaps *the righteous* refers to God. The saying would then mean that God observes the house of the righteous, but overthrows the wicked.

Verse 13: See also 14:31; 19:17.

Verse 14: Bribery is morally wrong, but its practical effectiveness cannot be denied.

Verse 15: In light of divine retribution, the righteous person rejoices and the wicked person laments.

Verse 16: The *assembly (company) of the dead* probably refers to Sheol, the eventual home of all persons.

Verse 17: Oil, used for bathing and anointing, could only be found in the homes of wealthier persons.

Verse 18: Synonymous parallelism conveys the message that the wicked suffer instead of the righteous.

Verse 19: See verse 9.

Verse 20: The business practices of the wise and the foolish are contrasted in this antithetical saying.

Verse 21: The rewards of a morally virtuous life are longevity and popular esteem.

Verse 22: Wisdom always exceeds political power and military might.

Verse 23: See also 12:13; 13:3.

Verse 24: The saying offers a clear definition of the scoffer: arrogant, self-centered, and vain.

Verse 25: See also 19:24.

Verse 26: Different senses of responsibility characterize righteous and wicked persons.

Verse 27: See 15:8.

Verse 28: The first line of this saying condemns perjury; the second line is too obscure to interpret.

Verse 29: The parallelism is unclear in this saying. An arrogant face reflects inward evil; the outward appearance of persons mirrors their heart.

Verse 30: Human wisdom amounts to little when it is used to challenge God.

Verse 31: Despite all military preparations, God is the true cause of victory.

The Proverbs of Solomon, XIII (22:1-16)

Verse 1: Personal reputation is more valuable than wealth. The parallelism is synonymous.

Verse 2: See also 29:13.

Verse 3: See 27:12.

Verse 4: Virtue (humility) and faith (*the fear of the* LORD) bring excellent rewards.

Verse 5: See 15:19.

Verse 6: Since parents are the early teachers of their children, advice to teach moral values early is directed to them.

Verse 7: Poverty gives birth to economic servitude; see also 10:2.

Verse 8: See also 11:31; the subject is divine retribution.

Verse 9: Compassion for the poor reaps great benefits.

Verse 10: Synonymous parallelism is used; the advice is to remove scoffers from society.

Verse 11: Kings delight in the friendship of virtuous persons; see also 16:13.

Verse 12: Here is another difficult Hebrew text. As translated in the NIV and NRSV, the saying confirms divine watchfulness and subsequent retribution, especially against the sinner.

Verse 13: Here is another humorous barb directed at the lazy fool. See also 21:25.

Verse 14: See also Proverbs 7.

Verse 15: Discipline is necessary to train children.

Verse 16: See verse 9.

§ § § § § § §

The Message of Proverbs 19:1–22:16

For the sages, kingship seems to be both socially and morally necessary, and it has political and military value as well. Moreover, the king is subject to divine providence, just as all other human beings are (see 20:18). Kings, too, are subject to the operations of the moral order of divine retribution. Therefore, it is particularly wrong for a king to be perverse (see 16:12). Kings are required to administer justice in legal dealings (16:10), and to always be fair and above reproach.

As organizers and maintainers of social order, kings are necessary. Without their wise leadership, society would deteriorate into chaos and anarchy. Sages established high standards of conduct for kings and made them responsible for their own behavior, just like everyone else. Along with the power of the king came responsibility, for the king set the pace for moral excellence.

§ § § § § § §

PART SIX

Proverbs 22:17–24:34

Introduction to These Chapters

Since the publication in 1923 of the Egyptian Instructions of Amenemope, biblical scholars have noted numerous parallels, both in form and in theme, between Proverbs 22:17–24:22 and the Egyptian document. Similarities in the introduction, in the expanded style of the standard two-line indicative saying, the almost precise count of thirty sayings, and the thematic content have led scholars to conclude that a Hebrew sage probably borrowed Amenemope's material to include in his own work.

Minor revisions were necessary to accomodate Israelite religion, and a few words were changed here and there. Such a practice among ancient Near Eastern sages was not uncommon, as many other such parallels exist among Egyptian, Mesopotamian, and Israelite wisdom materials. The international context of the wisdom movement brought together scribes from many nations. There was considerable exchange of ideas and literary styles, and there were lively debates.

During the monarchy and afterwards, Israel was doubtless a participant in these interchanges. It is, therefore, neither surprising nor dishonest that one sage borrows material from another sage. After all, wisdom's gifts were universal, bound neither by political boundaries nor by religious loyalties.

Here is an outline of this section.

I. Introduction (22:17-21)
II. The Thirty Sayings (22:22–24:34)
   A. Group one (22:22-29)
   B. Group two (23:1-35)
   C. Group three (24:1-34)

Introduction (22:17-21)

This opening section functions as an introduction, stating clearly the purpose of the teachings that follow. In both style and theme, it resembles Proverbs 1–9. Beginning with injunctions to pay attention and learn the lessons that follow, hearers are told that such wisdom leads to faith (verse 19) and to proper morality (verse 21). There must be no question in the hearer's mind that these words are effective words and that they will, in fact, lead a person in the "right" way. The authority of these words rests on the author, who is *wise*. Later, as the student practiced these virtues, their correctness proved true.

Group One (22:22-29)

Verses 22-23: See 14:31; 22:4. This admonition repeats earlier warnings against harassing the poor. The Lord always stands at their side, defending them. The imperative plus motive style is similar to that used in chapters 1–9.

Verses 24-25: See 15:1, 18. Quick-tempered angry people create social and interpersonal strife. On that account, they should be avoided. Prudent persons do not allow themselves to be trapped in their web of violence.

Verses 26-27: See 6:1; 11:15. Assuming the debts of another person may cost someone his or her own *bed* (that is, home).

Verse 28: See 23:10. A prudent person should respect the property of another (see also Deuteronomy 19:14).

Verse 29: A talented person will not long go unnoticed.

Group Two (23:1-35)

Verses 1-3: These verses contain three instructions that outwardly urge proper table etiquette when dining in the presence of royalty. But more is at stake here than good manners. In the presence of powerful persons, one's behavior is of utmost importance. Such persons exercise far-reaching influence over one's life, particularly when such "foods" as they offer may disguise their interior motives. Be wary of powerful persons!

Verses 4-5: This couplet cautions against becoming excessively preoccupied with accumulating material wealth. Its transitory and unstable character makes it undependable and unworthy of one's ultimate loyalty and effort. It can vanish in an instant, like a bird.

Verses 6-8: The message of this triplet is that one should avoid accepting gifts or favors (paid) from a miser or from anyone who selfishly calculates the costs. Such a greedy person is busy tallying up others' indebtedness to him, and one may be assured that none of his favors come cheaply. His food may cause indigestion, or worse.

Verse 9: Wise words are wasted on fools, since they lack the understanding with which to comprehend or to appreciate them.

Verses 10-11: See 17:5; 22:28. It is unwise to oppress the poor further or to exacerbate their misery; they have the Lord to defend them (to serve as their redeemer). The Hebrew word for *redeemer* refers to the person (usually a family member) whose responsibility it is to care for his kinsman's affairs or to avenge wrongful death.

Verse 12: This verse serves as an introduction. See 1:1-6; 5:1; 22:17.

Verses 13-14: See 13:24; 19:18. Corporal punishment may be necessary to discipline a strong-willed child who is misbehaving. The danger of losing the child to the realm of the dead more than justifies the extreme measures of physical punishment.

Verses 15-16: A teacher rejoices over the student who

has learned well the lessons of wisdom and acts virtuously.

Verses 17-18: See 14:27; 15:33. The person who lives in faith (*the fear of the* LORD) enjoys both longevity and abundant blessing. Also, persons of faith can anticipate some type of meaningful future, and they know that death will not erase their memory.

Verses 19-21: Excessive drinking and eating lead to undesirable states: drunkenness and impoverishment due to laziness, and drowsiness due to overeating. Firsthand experience provides ample evidence for avoiding inebriation and gluttony.

Verses 22-25: Obedient and respectful children bring joy and pride to their parents. When children seek wisdom and understanding and engage in righteous conduct, parents know that their teachings have not gone unnoticed, and that the child's welfare is assured.

Verses 26-28: These verses contain warnings against illicit sexual relations (see also 7:1-27).

Verses 29-35: This section is an exquisite, fully-developed unit describing in detail the ill effects of drunkenness. The interjections in verse 29 are almost rhetorical, since only a drunkard acts in such a way. The descriptions of strange hallucinatory visions and meaningless chatter aptly characterize one who is inebriated. The endless tossing and turning of one's equilibrium prevents rest. Loss of memory and insensitivity to pain add further to the pathetic plight. Definitely, this kind of behavior should be avoided at all costs.

Group Three (24:1-34)

Verses 1-2: See 3:31-32; 23:17. These verses advise the avoidance of evil companions. Although a new chapter begins here, the material is a continuation of the thirty sayings begun in 22:22.

Verses 3-4: In the ancient world, just as today, persons'

homes were actually extensions of themselves—an expression of who they were. Homes meant success, safety, and a source of pride. Using the imagery of a home, wisdom provides a person a real home instead of merely a tent or stone building. True knowledge furnishes comfortable furniture and luxurious decor to one's home.

Verses 5-6: See 11:14; 20:18. Wisdom surpasses physical might, both for an individual and for a nation. Warfare is no substitute for prudent counsel and dialogue.

Verse 7: The idea behind this saying is that wisdom is beyond the economic reach of the fool. So fools remain silent in the marketplace (city gate), knowing that they lack adequate resources with which to purchase knowledge.

Verses 8-9: Popular names given to evildoers are mischief makers, sinners, and scoffers.

Verses 10-12: Persons of true integrity come to the aid of their neighbors in distress; they are not deterred by difficult times nor by possible trouble stemming from involvement. By contrast, not even a plea of ignorance will excuse calculating cowards, for God knows their intentions and judges them accordingly.

Verses 13-14: The pleasant effects of wisdom are compared to the good taste of honey. But not only is wisdom satisfying in terms of a virtuous life, it also holds the key to longevity and blessedness. See also 16:24.

Verses 15-16: This admonition advises against doing violence to the homes of righteous persons, for their protection from God is endless and unbreachable. Such folly can only bring disaster for the perpetrator.

Verses 17-18: Divine punishment of the enemy should not be the cause of one's celebration; the Lord's wrath may be turned away from the enemy and toward you! There is no great theological lesson here. The motive is purely utilitarian.

Verses 19-20: See verses 1 and 14. The fate of the

evildoer is sudden death and extinction. Whatever may be the nature of the future, it is a matter of no importance for the evildoer, who has no future.

Verses 21-22: Proper respect for authority—divine and royal—is advised here. Dire consequences result from disobeying either one.

Verse 23: A new section of sayings is introduced here. The *thirty sayings* (22:20) are completed with verse 22.

Verses 23-26: See 18:5. Fairness within the judicial system is rewarded not only by favorable public acclaim, but with abundant blessings as well. Truthfulness may be sealed by the kiss of friendship.

Verse 27: Before marrying and rearing a family, one's economic situation must be attended to and made secure.

Verses 28-29: See 14:25; 20:22. Perjury, even against one's enemy, is morally wrong. Allow divine retribution its proper prerogative.

Verses 30-34: See 6:6-11. These verses contain further warnings against laziness.

§ § § § § § §

The Message of Proverbs 22:17–24:34

Most Old Testament scholars concur that Proverbs is a manual for ethical instruction. The sayings were collected and presented in order that generations of students might learn to distinguish righteousness and wisdom from evil and folly. Much of the material appears here because of its practical nature. It gives sound advice or teaches valuable lessons. Youth, especially, can be and should be taught right behavior—it does not come naturally.

There are also many sayings in Proverbs that emphasize purity of intent, rather than merely outward consequence. In 16:2, the Lord is described as weighing the spirit (NRSV) which means understanding the true motives of the heart (NIV). In 20:12 God created not only the outward senses, but the inward spirit as well. In 21:2 the Lord *weighs the heart.* Outward behavior is only one criteria for ethical evaluation—motive must also be taken into account in determining the virtue of an act.

In short, the ethics of Proverbs are much more complex and sophisticated than might be imagined. The Israelite sages established several criteria for assessing the moral worth (or worthlessness) of human behavior. Traditional categories of philosophical ethics must be used with caution in analyzing Proverbs. The sayings in Proverbs come from many hands, reflect many ethical criteria, and urge many patterns of conduct deemed "wise." Both the ends and the means are important elements in righteous conduct.

§ § § § § § §

Introduction to These Chapters

These chapters contain more proverbs of Solomon.
They may be outlined as follows.

Superscription (25:1)

The editors of the final version of Proverbs included a
second major collection in the book, similar in style and
content to chapters 10–24. Specifically, this second
collection is attributed to the men of Hezekiah, king of
Judah (715–687 B.C.). Scribal support from the royal
throne stimulated scholarly work among the sages,
including composing, editing, and copying sayings.
Many themes in this second collection appeared earlier in
chapter 10.

Group One (25:2-28)

Verse 2: See 16:10. This proverb discloses an interesting
and insightful comparison: the intentional
mysteriousness of divine activity versus perceptive
discernment by the king. Part of the value of a king is his
ability to unravel complicated legal and social problems,

and perhaps even to discern the divine will. This proverb is antithetical.

Verse 3: The superior wisdom of a king is limitless, just as are the heights of heaven and the depths of earth. See verse 2.

Verses 4-5: Just as a craftsman molds a fine vessel from refined metal, separated from its impurities, so a king's rule of his kingdom improves with the elimination of wrongdoers. Society improves as wickedness declines.

Verses 6-7b: This saying deals with social standing and royal patronage. It warns against attempting to elevate one's place in the social order by self-machinations. It is better to allow the king to recognize and reward a person than to aggressively curry his favor, only to be denied, rejected, and relegated to a lower status.

Verses 7c-10: Persons should not judge on the basis of appearances—matters may not be as they appear. Likewise, they should not disclose items confided to them—as would a gossiper. Loss of public esteem is too high a price for such imprudent acts. Disputes should be settled privately and out of court (verse 9).

Verse 11: Both a poorly preserved Hebrew text and confusing syntax contribute to make this saying difficult to translate. As it stands in the NIV and NRSV, the saying compliments timely and appropriate speech. See 15:23. This proverb is comparative.

Verse 12: Comparisons are effective pedagogical instruments and are of considerable artistic worth. Here, a good adviser to someone in need of counsel is compared to costly jewelry; both are of immense value.

Verse 13: A trustworthy and responsible messenger is a valuable asset to a community (see also 13:17). The services the messengers perform are essential to the survival of the group. Similarly, the cool waters from melted snow refresh workers during harvest season.

Verse 14: A sense of disappointment arises from promising weather conditions that fail to produce needed rain. Likewise, persons are usually frustrated by unfulfilled promises made by a braggart. This proverb is comparative.

Verse 15: Patience and prudence are two important virtues; they are effective, even to the point of accomplishing seemingly impossible tasks. The parallelism is synonymous.

Verse 16: On the surface, this saying urges moderation in satisfying one's appetite, particularly with tasty and rich foods. More generally, caution is urged for anything that seems too "good."

Verse 17: Even friendship and neighborliness have saturation points. Care must be exercised in order for persons not to "wear out their welcome."

Verse 18: Lying is particularly wicked because of the terrible consequences it can bring. Note the reference to common weapons of war. (See also 14:25.) The parallelism is comparative.

Verse 19: Dependability is the theme of this comparative saying. A bad tooth, a clumsy foot, and misplaced trust are all unreliable.

Verse 20: Three behaviors that only worsen situations are pouring vinegar onto a wound (NRSV; NIV = *soda*), removing clothing in cold weather, and singing to cheer a person who is depressed. None do any real good.

Verses 21-22: Kindness to one's enemy brings pangs of conscience to the enemy and blessings from the Lord. Again, the act is judged "good" on the basis of consequences—not by motives. See also Romans 12:20.

Verse 23: Although the reference to Palestinian weather conditions is unclear, the sense of the saying is that slander and a vicious tongue invite scorn and disapproval. Perhaps rains caused by a north wind were equally unwelcome. The parallelism is synonymous.

Verse 24: See 21:9.

Verse 25: See 15:30; 25:13. Just as a drink of water

refreshes the body, so does good news lift up one's spirits. The proverb is comparative.

Verse 26: Particularly distressing is the virtuous person who has turned to wickedness—just like tasty spring water that has become muddy or a fountain that streams forth impure water.

Verse 27: See verse 16. Too much of a good thing is dangerous—whether it is honey or flattering speech.

Verse 28: See 16:32; 17:27; 18:13. A quick temper causes persons to utter words that they may later regret, and that make them vulnerable, or open to counterattack.

Group Two (26:1-28)

Verse 1: Summers are hot in Palestine and harvest months are dry. To alter these established patterns with unexpected snow and rain would be devastating. Likewise, high honor bestowed upon a fool would be totally inappropriate. See also 19:10. The parallelism is comparative.

Verse 2: This comparison is extremely interesting and subtle. Just as a sparrow flits about from perch to perch without landing, and a swallow moves around aimlessly, a curse that is uttered for insufficient cause has no real power—it is ineffective.

Verse 3: See 10:13; 19:29. This verse contains alternative methods of corrective instructions.

Verse 4: One should not respond to fools using their own language, since this is actually sinking to the same level as the fool. The style here is that of negative instruction.

Verse 5: This verse is antithetical to verse 4. One should answer fools in their own language, to show them the folly of their ways.

Verse 6: See 13:17; 25:13. To use unreliable messengers is to invite trouble.

Verse 7: Lame persons can make no use of their bad limbs; fools have no use for proverbs, because they lack understanding. See also 17:16. The parallelism is comparative.

Verse 8: A stone that is wrapped too tightly in the sling cannot be thrown, and thus is useless. Likewise, honor bestowed upon the fool is equally without value. See also 26:1. The parallelism is comparative.

Verse 9: This proverb describes two situations that are potentially harmful: a briar in the hand of a drunk and a proverb in the mouth of a fool. Again, the parallelism is comparative.

Verse 10: This saying is virtually too corrupt, textually, for translation. In the NIV and NRSV it suggests the dangers resulting from a lack of purposive and planned action—shooting arrows wildly and hiring helpers who are fools or drunks.

Verse 11: Being ignorant, some creatures never learn from their mistakes; they repeat their folly over and over again.

Verse 12: Self-centered arrogance spells disaster for a person, more than even the folly of the fool.

Verse 13: See also 22:13. This verse is a humorous barb at the *sluggard* (NIV; NRSV = *lazy person*), who uses imaginary fears to avoid work.

Verse 14: Sluggards never go anywhere or accomplish anything; they just rock back and forth on their beds, like a door on hinges.

Verse 15: See 19:24. The sluggard is too lazy even to eat.

Verse 16: A false arrogance also characterizes sluggards—they think themselves wiser than the wisest.

Verse 17: This is good advice for anyone; if you did not start a quarrel, then stay out of it. It could be dangerous—stray dogs bite strangers. The proverb uses comparative parallelism.

Verses 18-19: Practical jokes or thoughtless teasing directed at one's neighbors could backfire and cause unnecessary strife.

Verse 20: Just as a fire requires fuel in order to burn, so also does an argument.

Verse 21: See verse 20.

Verse 22: See 18:8.

Verse 23: See 10:18. Outward appearances may be enticing, yet conceal inward malice. Flowery talk merely covers an evil heart. The parallelism is comparative.

Verses 24-26: Wicked persons often conceal their malice with attractive words. But they cannot disguise forever their real intent. Sooner or later, their wickedness will be exposed publicly.

Verse 27: A clear statement of natural retribution—for every act, there is a corresponding consequence. Evil begets evil. The proverb uses synonymous parallelism.

Verse 28: A liar clearly intends to deceive his hearers, thereby revealing an attitude of contempt toward them. To mislead another person intentionally indicates a truly gross form of disrespect. Similarly, one who lavishes compliments is possibly setting up a victim for a vicious attack.

Group Three (27:1-27)

Verse 1: With the uncertainty of the future, persons are well-advised to be cautious in their boastful predictions; things may not turn out as they expect. The proverb is in the style of a negative admonition.

Verse 2: It is better that another person express praise toward you than that you brag about yourself. For both social and psychological reasons, no one likes conceit. The parable uses synonymous parallelism.

Verse 3: Anger (*provocation*) is of greater force than either stone or sand, because it is more aggressive and dangerous. Unchecked emotions can cause greater damage than heavy, but inert, elements.

Verse 4: While wrath and anger are certainly dangerous emotions, jealousy outweighs both of them. An outraged spouse completely loses control and burns forever. The proverb is in the form of a rhetorical question.

Verse 5: The *hidden love* probably refers to corrective love. Thus, the saying suggests that a word of correction is better than ignoring a fault, under the pretense of love. The proverb is comparative.

Verse 6: See verse 5. Good friends are able to offer help and correction even though it may cause hurt; an enemy only flatters and allows persons to perpetuate the folly. The proverb uses antithetical parallelism.

Verse 7: To a person with a full stomach, not even delicious food tastes good; but even bitter herbs are tasty to one who is hungry. The parallelism is antithetical.

Verse 8: Danger, anxieties of relocation, and a sense of loss come to persons (or animals) who wander away from their homes. The parallelism is comparative.

Verse 10: The logical connections among these triplets are difficult to discern; the general idea of verse 10*a* is to remain loyal to family friends during adversity. Yet verse 10*b* seems to suggest that even a brother is little help in time of trouble. Much better is a dependable friend (verse 10*c*) than a brother who remains afar. The proverb is comparative.

Verse 11: Since teachers are often judged by their students, a pupil who has learned his or her lessons will enable a teacher to establish and preserve accountability. The style is admonition.

Verse 12: See also 22:3.

Verse 13: See also 20:16.

Verse 14: A pretentious, untimely display of friendship must be met with suspicion. Insincerity is a form of profanity.

Verses 15-16: See 9:13*b*. An irritable woman is tiresome as well as troublesome. It is futile to try and soothe her irritation.

Verse 17: Acknowledging the social nature of human beings, this saying affirms the value of personal interaction. Just as iron sharpens iron, interaction among persons stimulates thoughts, feelings, and behaviors. Synonymous parallelism is used.

Verse 18: Industriousness and loyalty are virtues that engender great rewards. The parallelism is synonymous.

Verse 19: The mirror effect of clear water is similar to the way a person's behavior reflects his or her true self. In a real sense, as human beings, what we do mirrors who we are. The parallelism is synonymous.

Verse 20: Just as the realms of death and destruction (*Sheol* and *Abaddon*) possess insatiable appetites, human desires can never be satisfied. The more wealth we have, the more we need and want. Synonymous parallelism is used.

Verse 21: The first line is identified with 17:3*a*—the crucible and the furnace are where precious metals are formed. The second line may have either of two meanings: Persons are judged by their reputations, or they are judged by what they value (*praise*).

Verse 22: Not even the most drastic measures will remove the folly from a fool.

Verses 23-27: The virtues of agrarian life are fully sufficient for the well-being of persons. The necessities of life are all available to persons who remain on the farm.

Group Four (28:1-28)

Verse 1: Clarity of purpose and moral integrity empower the righteous person with courage, while the evildoer slinks away in cowardly fear. The style is antithetical.

Verse 2: Political instability, indicated by a constant succession of leaders, may be considered as being national punishment. By contrast, the Lord blesses a righteous nation with able and stable leadership. The parallelism is antithetical.

Verse 3: A ruler who oppresses the poor can make their miserable plights even worse. Similarly, a torrential downpour sweeps away everything in its path, leaving a land barren.

Verse 4: The word translated *law* (Hebrew *torah*) may refer either to the Mosaic law (13:13) or to the instruction of the wise (1:8); both translations are possible. In either case, obedience to the law (or instruction) means actively opposing evil.

Verse 5: Wickedness prevents one from understanding the need for and nature of social justice; that is, it makes one totally self-centered. Persons of faith respect the rights and privileges of others.

Verse 6: See also 19:1. Even though they may be poor, persons of integrity are to be preferred over wealthy persons who are evil. The proverb is antithetical.

Verse 7: As in verse 4, the word *law* may have a double meaning: Mosaic law or moral instruction. *Gluttons* are persons who live only to satisfy their insatiable appetites. The proverb uses antithetical parallelism.

Verse 8: Charging *exhorbitant interest* is judged as wrong in the Old Testament. And such illf-gotten gain will eventually pass on to one who is just and compassionate.

Verse 9: See verses 4 and 7 for *law*. Prayers or other expressions of piety are judged as hypocritical, unless they are accompanied by obedience to law or moral instruction.

Verse 10: See 26:27. Retribution befalls whoever causes the righteous to sin. This is an antithetical proverb.

Verse 11: Economic success may lead to arrogance and conceit, both of which are clearly visible to a person with wisdom. Antithetical parallelism is used.

Verse 12: The interpretation of this saying is problematic. The saying probably contrasts the universal joy that accompanies righteous success with the public withdrawal away from wicked persons.

Verse 13: Confession and correction of moral wrongdoing are met with divine mercy, but those who try to conceal their sin force divine judgment. The parallelism is antithetical.

Verse 14: The NIV adds the Lord as the object of the verb *fear* (see also 15:33). Actually, the fear may refer instead to the sense of respect for the moral order, especially in view of the parallelism in the second line. The proverb is antithetical.

Verse 15: Running out of control and causing terrible devastation, an evil ruler (like wild beasts) inflicts needless pain and suffering upon defenseless victims. The style of this proverb is comparative.

Verse 16: The Hebrew text is far less clear than the NIV and NRSV translations suggest. Perhaps the saying contrasts the cruelty of an unwise ruler with the civility of wise rule, but this is only an educated guess as to the meaning.

Verse 17: This Hebrew text is again impossible to translate. As it stands in the NIV and NRSV, it alludes to the incurring of bloodguilt and how the bearer may be pursued for life, with none to help him.

Verse 18: See 10:9. The theme is divine retribution.

Verse 19: See 12:11.

Verse 20: Quick riches improperly acquired are short-lived, as contrasted with the longevity resulting from faithfulness and righteousness. The style is antithetical.

Verse 21: See 24:23b for line one. The second line suggests how little it takes to tempt some persons to do wrong—including even a corrupt judge.

Verse 22: Greed and selfishness lead a person to disastrous results; one's misconceptions about wealth will eventually work to one's own detriment.

Verse 23: See 27:5-6; 29:5. Honesty, rather than flattery, is the sign of true friendship.

Verse 24: Children who surreptitiously attempt to secure their parents' wealth as a rightful but early inheritance commit a terrible sin.

Verse 25: Greed, as a means of satisfying one's wants, is contrasted with trust in the Lord to provide for one's needs. The proverb is antithetical.

Verse 26: Conceit and arrogance lead persons to ignore good counsel and wisdom, and hence lead them toward destruction. A wise person knows full well human limitations. The proverb is antithetical.

Verse 27: See 19:17. Generosity and compassion toward the poor earn one divine favor; greed and selfishness bring punishment. This is an antithetical proverb.

Verse 28: See 29:2. In the face of wicked rulers subjects disappear; when a righteous leader assumes control, subjects reappear. The antithetical style is used.

Group Five (29:1-27)

Verse 1: Permanent disaster awaits the person who refuses to heed warnings and to listen to wise counsel.

Verse 2: See 16:10-15; 28:12, 28. The subject is the popularity of a righteous ruler, and the style is antithetical.

Verse 3: See 10:1; 5:1-23. A child receptive to the wise teachings of a father knows to avoid illicit sexual relations. The parallelism is antithetical.

Verse 4: See verse 2. The subject is the benefits of a just king.

Verse 5: See 26:28; 28:23. Flattery is sheer deception! It should not be uttered, nor should it be paid attention to. The phrase *his feet* (NIV) may belong either to the flatterer or the one being flattered (NRSV = *neighbor's feet*).

Verse 6: In view of the trustworthy operations of the moral order, wicked persons will become entangled in their own web of violence. Righteous persons rejoice in their freedom and happiness. The antithetical style is used.

Verse 7: See 14:21; 22:22-23. The rights of the poor are underwritten and guaranteed, ultimately, by the Lord. A wise person knows this, and acts accordingly. The parallelism is antithetical.

Verse 8: See 26:20-21. *Scoffers* (*mockers*) or troublemakers stir up popular dissent and fracture a society, whereas wise persons bring peace and calm to a city. Antithetical parallelism is used.

Verse 9: An argument, or perhaps a lawsuit, with a fool is probably futile; either he ridicules his opponent ceaselessly, or else he tries to gloss over the issue with laughter.

Verse 10: Morally righteous persons may be the objects of enmity and threats from evildoers. The jealousy of the latter produces hatred toward the former.

Verse 11: See 16:32; 25:28. The wisdom of self-control is the subject of this proverb.

Verse 12: The moral climate of a community is established by the leaders of that community; as the king does, so do his subjects.

Verse 13: See 22:2. Both the powerful and the oppressed come together as creatures given breath by the Lord; God made them both.

Verse 14: See also 16:12; 20:28. Royal justice ensures political stability.

Verse 15: On 15*a* see 23:13-14. On 15*b*, see 10:1; 17:25. Children need moral instruction from their parents. The style of the proverb is antithetical.

Verse 16: See verse 2. Violence and oppression from political leadership actually increase criminal activity, but divine retribution ensures that eventually justice will prevail. The parallelism is antithetical.

Verse 17: See 22:6; 29:15. Educating a child well results not only in a righteous and successful life for the child, but also in a state of peace and satisfaction for the parents.

Verse 18: Divine guidance (referred to as *prophecy* or *revelation*) provides order and stability in society, just as the *law* (or instruction) brings blessings. *Prophecy* refers to the second section of the Hebrew canon and the *law* is the first division.

Verse 19: Slaves (*servants*) in the ancient Near East were generally considered to be of minimal intelligence; thus they were practically impossible to educate without sterner measures than would be used ordinarily. They lacked the necessary knowledge to understand.

Verse 20: See 17:27; 26:12. A hasty, ill-conceived response often causes serious trouble. Persons should think before they speak.

Verse 21: The second line of this couplet is difficult to translate. In the NIV and NRSV, the saying suggests that servants who are reared improperly will forever need the care and financial support of their master.

Verse 22: See also 15:18. The subject is the dangers of unchecked anger. The parallelism is synonymous.

Verse 23: See 11:2; 15:33; 16:18; 18:12. Pride and humility are contrasted. The proverb uses antithetical parallelism.

Verse 24: See Leviticus 5:1. Concealing information regarding criminal activity implicates a person in the crime legally and morally.

Verse 25: This saying is brilliant in its insight into human psychology. Fear can totally immobilize persons, causing them to self-destruct. By contrast, faith is a source of strength and confidence, giving persons the courage to act. The proverb is antithetical.

Verse 26: Ultimately, justice and blessings proceed from the Lord, not from a ruler. Antithetical parallelism is used here.

Verse 27: The righteous and the wicked possess a mutual antipathy toward each other.

§ § § § § § §

The Message of Proverbs 25–29

The message of this section of Proverbs is based on the general assumption that God is revealed in various ways, including the law (28:4, 7 ,9), prophecy (29:18), and the teachings of wisdom (1:20-33).

The law (Hebrew *torah*) generally refers to the Pentateuch, or the first five books in the Old Testament. Because of its traditional authority in Jewish thought, the Law occupies a position of supremacy in the canon. The concepts of election (God's special choice of Israel as a means of grace) and exodus (freedom and redemption) provided ancient Israel with a sense of theological identity and purpose. The laws the people received at Mount Sinai distinguished them from other peoples, and provided a means by which they satisfied their obligation to the Lord.

In the prophetic literature, Israel's theologians recorded their interpretations of God's operations in the histories of Israel and Judah. Divine leadership came through the mouth of prophets, called aside to deliver a unique word. Then in the Wisdom Literature, the sages claimed God's will could be discerned through the natural and moral orders. Righteous conduct always met divine approval while folly ended in divine judgment.

§ § § § § § §

Proverbs 30–31

Introduction to These Chapters

This chapter has two main parts.
I. The Words of Agur (30:1-9)
II. Instructions and Numerical Sayings (30:10-33)
III. The Words of Lemuel (31:1-9)
IV. The Ideal Wife (31:10-31)

The Words of Agur (30:1-9)

This brief dialogue comes from a certain man by the name of Agur, the son of Jakeh (verse 1). Agur's home is identified as Massa, a region located northeast of Palestine on the edge of the Arabian desert (see Genesis 25:14; 1 Chronicles 1:30). Agur is mentioned only here in the Old Testament, so nothing else is known about him. His homeland and his name suggest that he, like Job, is non-Israelite. The nature of his concern suggests a period long after the ideas in Proverbs 10:1–22:16 had been crystalized. Confidence in wisdom's gifts had begun to diminish.

In verses 1-4, Agur raises important questions about the limits of human knowledge and claims a certain ignorance in regard to the affairs of God as mediated through the natural and moral orders. Verses 5-6 respond with injunctions to avoid such heretical questions for fear of divine retribution.

The opening phrases in verse 1b are too problematic in the Hebrew text to translate accurately. The NIV reads

This man declared to Ithiel, to Ithiel and Ucal. The Greek translation of the Old Testament takes *ithiel* as a verb phrase meaning, *There is no God*, so that the section opens with an explicit denial of divine existence. This is followed in the Greek version by a confession of sheer exhaustion in the face of futile efforts to find God: *I am exhausted.* However, the NIV and NRSV do not follow this Greek translation. The NRSV, based on a different word division of the Hebrew, has *I am weary, O God. How can I prevail?*

Verses 2-3 are a self-effacing comment, probably intended sarcastically or perhaps as ironic. Agur realizes that there are strict limits to human understanding, and that a person's knowledge of God may be small, indeed. These ideas challenge the basic notions of other parts of Proverbs which claim that knowledge of God and God's ways is offered by wisdom (1:20-33). Agur claims that he lacks the kind of wisdom that played before God (8:1-36), learning the secrets of Creation.

The rhetorical questions in verse 4 contain considerable mythological imagery. The mythical chariot ride into the heavens (4*a*), gathering wind in a hand (4*b*), wrapping waters in a garment (4*c*), the son of God (4*d*)—all these images are found in Mesopotamian and Canaanite mythological texts. The literary talent of Agur certainly matched well the profundity of his theme. Only God, he suggests, knows the answers to ultimate questions such as these. And, judging from verses 2-3, God has not chosen to share these answers with persons on earth. Hence, the assumption of wisdom about our natural knowledge of divine affairs is called into question.

But Agur's reception is challenged by the confession of faith in verses 5-9. Here, the faith of human beings in divine revelation is reaffirmed and the skeptic is chastened (verses 5-6). In faith—if not in actual experience—God's faithfulness to obedient servants is reaffirmed.

The faithful respondent then adds a final request of the Lord—make him truthful and provide for his basic needs. Too much affluence might lead to arrogance or conceit, and too little money might lead to acts of dishonesty.

Instructions and Numerical Sayings (30:10-33)

Verse 10: This negative injunction urges caution in falsifying information about a slave (*servant*) to his master. The slander may be discovered, and the master would then vent his anger against the perpetrator.

Verses 11-14: These verses discuss four kinds of wicked persons. The sages find certain types of evil persons particularly vile:

(1) those who curse their parents (that is, show disrespect for them);

(2) hypocrites;

(3) conceited and arrogant persons;

(4) persons who oppress the poor.

Notice that no motive-clauses are attached to these acts, nor is mention made of their consequences. These immoral acts are all inherently evil.

Verses 15-16: These verses describe four things that can never be satisfied. The numerical saying is a particularly attractive literary form, and one that could be easily memorized. The three-and-four pattern (see also Amos 1–2) suggests the large number of behaviors that are characterized here. In this quatrain, the sage describes four things whose appetites are insatiable—(1) Sheol (*the grave*), (2) a barren womb, (3) a dry earth, and (4) an unquenched fire. The unit is introduced by a saying about a leech, who never seems to be sated.

Verse 17: This saying describes figuratively the terrible consequences resulting from disobeying one's parents (see 30:11). This verse has no literary or conceptual relationship to verse 16 or verse 18.

Verses 18-19: The writer describes four amazing and marvelous states of affairs: (1) how the majestic eagle soars above earth supported only by its wings; (2) how the snake moves about with no visible means of locomotion; (3) how a heavy ship stays afloat on the seas; and (4) the attraction between a man and a woman.

Verse 20: The adulteress considers her immoral acts as merely satisfying her physical appetites, like eating food. She completely lacks a moral conscience. (See also 5:1-23.)

Verses 21-23: These verses describe four intolerable circumstances: (1) whenever a slave (*servant*) becomes a king—he will abuse the powers of his office; (2) whenever the physical appetites of a fool are satisfied—he only lives for the gratification of the moment; (3) whenever a lonely woman finds a husband—she becomes arrogant and possessive; and (4) whenever a maid displaces her mistress—pride causes her to become indignant toward her former owner.

Verses 24-28: Four things are small but wise: (1) ants, deceptively small, but diligent and competent in providing food for future days; (2) rock-badgers or *coneys*, which are weak animals, but survive in barren places that other creatures avoid; (3) locusts that discipline themselves to work in organized patterns; and (4) lizards, small but agile, which can maneuver into royal palaces.

Verses 29-31: Four creatures are imposing in their presence: (1) a lion, brave and fearless; (2) a strutting rooster (translation uncertain); (3) a he-goat; and (4) a king, parading before his subjects.

Verses 32-33: These verses advise to ease up on pressure and anger. Too much pressure on milk causes it to curdle; too much pressure on the nose causes it to bleed; too much anger causes personal and social disruption. Likewise, too much foolishness or arrogance causes trouble, so one should ease up and back off.

The Words of Lemuel (31:1-9)

Verse 1: The superscription ascribes authorship of these instructions to the mother of Lemuel, king of Massa. Lemuel is mentioned only here in the Old Testament. For Massa see 30:1.

Verse 2: Rhetorical questions introduce her instructions to her son—*What am I to say to you, my son?* What indeed?

Verses 3-7: This mother begins her words to her son by warning him to avoid evil women who would lead him astray and weaken his moral leadership (see 5:1 and following). She continues by urging him to restrain from intoxicants that result in memory loss or in perversions of justice. Royal leadership cannot afford either of these consequences. Instead, wine should be given to persons who are suffering in order to ease their misery—either physical misery or economic misery. Dulled senses ease pain!

Verses 8-9: The king is urged to defend the rights of those who cannot defend themselves, either because they are weak or because they are poor. As the preserver of social justice, the king must help those persons who are unable to help themselves.

The Ideal Wife (31:10-31)

Throughout the book of Proverbs, wives have been the object of both praise and judgment. In 19:14, a good wife is described as coming from the Lord. She is instrumental in training children and youth. Her contributions to the family are of the greatest importance. But wives can also be the object of judgment. They can nag (21:9); they can be quarrelsome (21:19). But worst of all they can be unfaithful (7:19).

To conclude this book of moral teaching, the editor of Proverbs includes a beautiful poem, detailing the virtues of an ideal wife. Clearly this is a self-contained literary unit with little relation to its setting in the book. Each verse of the poem begins with a consecutive letter of the

Hebrew alphabet. Thus, both in form and content, this elegant tribute to a wife establishes a high standard of conduct and describes the incomparable worth of a woman of virtue.

Verse 10: A good wife is scarce and of truly great value. The rhetorical question is somewhat misleading; it refers to the great difficulty of finding such a wife.

Verse 11: Her husband has complete trust and confidence in her.

Verse 12: His trust is vindicated by the fact that she always acts rightly and appropriately.

Verse 13: She is diligent in seeing that her family is well clothed.

Verse 14: Her home is always well-stocked with food, both domestic and imported; her family will not go hungry.

Verse 15: She works early in the morning, probably baking bread for her family.

Verse 16: She is adroit at both real estate and agriculture.

Verse 17: She maintains her health and exudes abundant energy.

Verse 18: She is shrewd in business and is not lazy or indolent in her other affairs.

Verse 19: She makes clothing for her family (see also verse 13).

Verse 20: She attends to the needs of the poor, with a sense of social responsibility.

Verse 21: Bad weather does not frighten her since her family is well-protected by warm clothing.

Verse 22: See verse 13. She is a seamstress.

Verse 23: Because of her good management of the household, her husband is free to pursue other matters elsewhere and enjoy dialogue with the important men of the community who gather at the city gate.

Verse 24: See verse 22.

Verse 25: She remains charming, poised, and good-natured.

Verse 26: She is wise and kind.

Verse 27: She looks after her family, properly and diligently.

Verse 28: She receives properly the praise, love, and esteem of her family.

Verse 29: She is truly one of a kind.

Verse 30: Her faith surpasses even her charm and her beauty.

Verse 31: Give her full credit for all she does and allow her to be praised by everyone. She truly is an ideal wife.

§ § § § § § §

The Message of Proverbs 30–31

In a book that serves as the standard for divine retribution in the Old Testament, the words of Agur appear shocking and certainly out of place. To question wisdom's disclosure of divine knowledge, including the paths of moral righteousness, strikes at the very heart of wisdom theology.

Agur confesses his ignorance of wisdom, that is, the knowledge that comes from God. But even more disturbing is his belief that other persons are likewise ignorant. No one really has journeyed up to heaven and returned! No one can collect the winds and hold them in a clenched fist. No one can except God. Such knowledge is not possible for humans—not even the sages.

In many respects, we share Agur's doubts. Rabbi Kushner's best-seller, *When Bad Things Happen to Good People*, is ample testimony to popular mistrust in Proverbs' belief that the righteous prosper and the wicked suffer. Often, our actual experiences do not confirm wisdom theology and its notion of retribution. Job and Ecclesiastes had difficulty reconciling the experience of human suffering with wisdom's doctrine of retribution.

But Agur did not have the last word, for the final verses (5-9) respond well to his doubts. Only within the embrace of faith can one find understanding to confront (if not explain) human limitations on the knowledge of God's ways. Belief in divine retribution is a confession of faith, not a description of empirical facts. Agur's objections are offset by the only refutation possible—a confession of faith. For within faith, the Lord provides comfort and promise.

§ § § § § § §

Introduction to Ecclesiastes

The book of Ecclesiastes is certainly one of the most fascinating books in the Old Testament. Yet, when one begins reading, one may well wonder exactly how such a book came to be included in the Old Testament. After all, the author does not believe in divine retribution. He feels that there is no real profit to be gained from work on earth. And even worse, divine revelation is altogether scarce—if available at all. This material certainly differs radically from Proverbs and from most other books in the Old Testament.

Yet, for all of its differences, this small book contains some of the most intriguing reading in the Bible. The issues of doubt and pessimism it raises are issues that many persons confront day after day. The book truthfully concedes that goodness is not always rewarded tangibly, and evildoers are not always punished. Scarcely a thoughtful person has not wondered on occasion whether human existence has any real meaning or purpose. But the inclusion of Ecclesiastes within the Hebrew canon suggests that the content is worthy of examination.

The Author of the Book

According to the superscription (1:1), the book belongs to Qoheleth, the son of David, King in Jerusalem. The name *Qoheleth* is probably a personal name, although the grammatical form of the Hebrew word (a feminine participle) may also refer to an office or position such as a *teacher*. The word *Qoheleth* means *one who speaks in an assembly*, referring to a function rather than to a specific person. If the Hebrew word refers to a position rather than to a proper name, it should be translated as *the speaker*. When Martin Luther translated this book, he translated *Qoheleth* as *the preacher*; however, because of Qoheleth's theological scepticism, he can hardly be called a preacher.

Moreover, it is clear that the author assumes the identity of King Solomon, since he was the only son of David who was ever king in Jerusalem. To be sure, this Solomonic pseudonym is appropriate in view of Solomon's patronage of wisdom in his royal court. To affix such a famous name to a book guaranteed almost instant acceptance among the scribes, and was not really considered plagiarism at that time.

What, really, do we know about Qoheleth? In terms of concrete biographical data, we know nothing. But judging from the style and content of his writing, this person had extensive training in the wisdom tradition, and quite possibly was a sage himself. He writes with an almost intimate knowledge of basic wisdom notions such as retribution, morality, the righteous versus the wicked, proper speech, and so forth. He quotes many traditional proverbs, and occasionally adds his own peculiar words of scepticism. Also, in the conclusion, the final editors refer to Qoheleth as having taught knowledge and arranged proverbs with great care (12:9).

Here is a sage who has carefully weighed his real-life experience against his wisdom theology only to find the latter wanting. As the years pass, his pessimism deepens about the possibilities of human knowledge of God, including divine retribution. Finally, as he reaches his mature years, he submits his final legacy—his profound words of doubt—vanity of vanities, everything is vanity!

For the most part, this book represents Qoheleth's memoirs. Perhaps the superscription (1:1) and the conclusion (12:9-13) belong to another writer, and various proverbs from the wisdom tradition may have been included. But the great majority of the book belongs to Qoheleth.

The Date of the Book

The date of Qoheleth is approximately 250 B.C. The book contains numerous Aramaic words from the post-exilic era, shows considerable influence from Greek philosophy, and displays a full knowledge (and rejection) of mature wisdom theology.

On the other hand, a Qoheleth scroll found at Qumran indicates the inclusion of the book in the canon by mid-second century B.C. There are no concrete historical allusions in the book that reflect its date. So most scholars concur in dating the book after 300 B.C. but before 150 B.C.

Theological Themes in the Book

Qoheleth lacks a clear pattern of thematic development or even of logical consistency. Most efforts to trace the development of a common theme (such as vanity) are futile. The book contains too many tangents, overt contradictions, and repetitions. It is even difficult to prepare a basic outline of the book.

Qoheleth has compiled this book over a number of years, and several themes have been examined and reexamined from different points of view. This technique gives the work a certain redundancy and even outright contradictoriness. Traditional proverbs are juxtaposed with pessimistic conclusions drawn from experience (1:14-18). Poems precede narratives (1:1-11; 3:1-9).

But the rough, uneven style of the book reflects Qoheleth's perception of the rough, uneven, undirected nature of human existence. It is vain, he concludes, to try to understand the purpose and value of human existence. Instead, one should enjoy life as God gives it. Likewise, it is of no profit to try to discern a logical structure to his book. As Qoheleth advises persons to enjoy life and reap whatever benefits come along (2:24-26), so would he advise readers to examine his book, draw whatever lessons they may find appropriate, and not expect to solve the mysteries of the human existence by studying the pages of his reflections.

The basic theological ideas in Qoheleth's book challenge wisdom ideas in Proverbs, such as divine retribution, divine revelation communicated through the natural and moral order, wisdom as providing the way of understanding and succeeding in life, and our unique and exalted place in God's created order.

Qoheleth can find nothing in his experience to validate these ideas. Instead, he urges persons to enjoy life, accept their work as self-rewarding, and not expect complete understanding of God's ways. Morality—like faith—should be unconditional, that is, not based on anticipated rewards (or punishment). For life, even with all its perplexities, is still vastly superior to the alternative, death.

Ecclesiastes 1–3

Introduction to These Chapters

The first three chapters of Ecclesiastes may be divided into five parts.
  I. Superscription (1:1)
  II. Vanity of Vanities (1:2-11)
  III. Search for Meaning and Value (1:12–2:26)
  IV. Times and Seasons (3:1-15)
  V. Human Mortality and Divine Justice (3:16-22)

Superscription (1:1)

The book of Ecclesiastes opens with a superscription that identifies Qoheleth as the author and names him as the son of David, King in Jerusalem. Like most superscriptions in the Bible, this one is probably secondary. This guise of Solomonic kingship is followed only in the first two chapters; elsewhere Qoheleth is not a king (see 8:2).

Vanity of Vanities (1:2-11)

The central thesis of Qoheleth's book is the vanity of human existence. The Hebrew word for vanity is *hebel*, which more literally means *breath, vapor*—that is, empty or non-lasting. Human existence, he proclaims, is empty of all meaning, purpose, and value. Qoheleth then validates this thesis by various tests—power, pleasure, love, religion, and so forth. But from the very beginning, the reader is clear as to Qoheleth's central idea—*Vanity of vanity; all is vanity* (NRSV). The NIV expresses this idea in a different way: *Meaningless, meaningless. Everything is meaningless.* This phrase also concludes the book in 12:8.

Following this opening pessimistic statement, Qoheleth presents a brief poem on the endless, repetitive cycles of nature. Beginning with a rhetorical question, What do people gain from all their labor? Qoheleth then describes the monotonous repetitions both of history and of nature. People come, people go. The sun rises, the sun sets. The rivers all run to the sea, but it is never filled. What has been is what now is, and what will be has already happened.

Nothing new ever happens on earth. Making matters worse, there is no remembrance of former things, nor will there be any memory of present things in the future. Life plods onward daily, weekly, monthly, year after year—with no real comprehension of purpose or direction. And for what reason? No one knows! This endless coming into being and passing out of being leaves humans in a lowly place, with little or no role to play in a universe devoid of discernible meaning. So what do we gain from the toil of our existence—nothing! For all is vanity.

Search for Meaning and Value (1:12–2:26)

Assuming the imaginary role of a king (probably Solomon), Qoheleth describes his quest to discover meaning in human existence (verse 12). He begins by stating his method of approach, to let the reader know exactly how he intends to conduct his quest. He begins by using human reason, but quickly concludes that life is unhappy. As in the preceding poem (1:3-11), his journey ends on a negative note. Yet, it is a journey that he (and everyone else) must make for himself. But in the end, Qoheleth discovers that God has not dealt human beings a "good hand"—for it is an unhappy business that God has given us. All is vanity. To support this conclusion he has drawn from his own firsthand experience, Qoheleth cites a traditional proverb about the rigidity of nature— *What is crooked (twisted) cannot be made straight, and what is lacking cannot be counted* (1:15).

Making existence even more distressing (if this could be possible), Qoheleth finds that increasing one's knowledge merely increases one's sense of futility in achieving genuine meaning, purpose, or value. For securing real knowledge is about as likely to happen as capturing the wind (1:17). So his quest begins with his search for wisdom, using his reason (1:13, 16). But he soon discovers that this method is futile (1:15, 18).

Qoheleth's next venture (2:1-11) emphasizes pleasure—pure, sensual hedonism. He surrounds himself with typical sources of pleasure—good wine (2:3); large homes (2:4); vineyards, parks, groves, pools of water, servants, flocks (2:7); wealth, concubines (2:8); and so forth. Qoheleth holds back nothing from himself. Whatever was thought to bring a sense of meaning or purpose to life, he obtains it in full measure. But, alas, pleasure and wealth too are futile—they bring no real value. Perhaps the only element of reward comes from the actual effort used to obtain this wealth or to secure these pleasures. The benefit comes from "trying" and not from "getting."

Then Qoheleth turns to wisdom, to learn the moral nature of the universe and to learn the difference between righteousness and folly. For surely, he thinks, wisdom will bring life (see Proverbs 1:33). Using wisdom, Qoheleth does discover some values—at least the wise man knows where he is going (verse 14), whereas the fool stumbles along blindly.

There are some practical benefits to be gained from righteous behavior—some sense of direction. But even this small reward is canceled, ultimately, by the ever-present threat of death—a fate common to the wise person and to the fool (verse 14). In the face of this common fate, all distinctions between the righteous and the wicked blur into insignificance (verse 15). Also, there is no lasting memory of either the wise or the fool (verse 16). The doleful realization of this fate leads Qoheleth to a deep scepticism about the ultimate value of life.

Further disappointing Qoheleth, he discovers that he must leave what little profit he has managed to accumulate to someone after him, who has neither earned it nor deserves it (verse 21). So, Qoheleth concludes that life is filled with days of fruitless toil, endless pain, and meaningless work. Even at night, sleep does not come. Life is vanity (verse 23).

Nevertheless, life is still preferable to death. In the face of the misery of human existence, what should a person do? Die? Certainly not! Qoheleth urges persons to enjoy life, including work, without trying to discover its mysteries, for God gives it to us—exactly as it is. And somewhere, somehow (verse 26) the righteous and the wicked person receive their just rewards. Perhaps the sinner pays more than he should pay for his sins; this too is vanity.

Qoheleth advises us that justice is too much to expect out of life. In the final analysis, Qoheleth advocates an unconditional acceptance of life as it comes, or retribution without expecting fairness. It is vanity to claim ultimate knowledge or to condition one's behavior upon expected consequences. The act/consequence model of the sages in Proverbs is an unreliable model!

Times and Seasons (3:1-15)

This well-known poem on times and seasons exhibits Qoheleth's sensitivity for the predetermined cycles of human existence—both natural and social cycles. In infinite wisdom, God has preset the times and seasons of life—birth-death, planting-harvesting, warfare-peace, destruction-construction, and so forth. This rigid pattern of seasons provides a sense of security in the face of threatening chaos (see also Genesis 1:2).

But, on another level, a rigidly fixed scheme of nature means that persons lack the freedom (see Genesis 2) to participate in the operations of life. Persons also are part of this predetermined plan. Such a view of pre-established human limitation heightens Qoheleth's sense of anxiety. Humankind's exalted place in God's order of creation has fallen considerably.

For all of its independent literary richness and beauty, this poem must be interpreted in relationship to verses 10-15. Here Qoheleth explains that while God has indeed established a majestic order and *made everything beautiful (suitable) in its time*, God has also put a sense of infinite mystery (NIV = *eternity*; NRSV = *a sense of past and future*) into persons' minds, such that they cannot discover the meaning or purpose behind the events of history. It is better that persons enjoy life, accept God's gifts as they come (if they come), respect the order of creation, and fear God. For events occur and reoccur in predetermined patterns, and we are unable to discover the principle behind this system. In verse 15, the phrase *God seeks out what has gone by* (NRSV; NIV = *God will call the past to account*) refers to God's clear predilection for matters that have occurred previously.

Human Mortality and Divine Justice (3:16-22)

Amid this divinely predetermined scheme of things, Qoheleth discovers that experience may contradict the expected plan for earthly justice. He observes that wickedness occurs in the place of righteouness (verse 16) and that social justice is not automatic. Qoheleth then quotes the traditional response of a sage. *God will judge (bring to judgment) the righteous and the wicked.* Yet, he knows from his own experience that such a theoretical response is at sharp variance with reality. After all, are men and women really anything more than mere animals (verse 18)?

By lowering persons to the status of mere creatures, Qoheleth directs an intentional barb at wisdom's praise and elevation of persons. But for Qoheleth, humans and animals share the same fate—death. Who knows whether there is anything beyond death (verse 21)? For all we really know is that both persons and beasts return to the dust. Human mortality thereby robs God of the opportunity for divine justice.

Once again, Qoheleth concludes that in the face of this perplexing unfairness in human existence, persons should face life as it comes and enjoy their labors. For that is their divinely established position in the overall scheme of things. Persons have no knowledge of the future.

§ § § § § § §

The Message of Ecclesiastes 1–3

Four major theological themes emerge from the first three chapters in Ecclesiastes: (1) Human existence is devoid of any real meaning, purpose, or value; (2) God has predetermined nature and history, so that persons have no contributions to make, apart from mechanistic compliance; (3) God has chosen to conceal God's will from persons; and (4) human beings and animals share a common fate—death.

When Qoheleth proclaims boldly that all is meaningless (vanity) (1:2), he states a thesis that he then supports by way of real-life experiences in the remaining chapters. Qoheleth pursues the meaning of human existence by means of traditionally accepted ways—power, pleasure, wisdom, religion, and so forth—but yet all ways lead to the same conclusion: *All is vanity*. Human reason and experience contrast sharply with traditional Hebrew faith, especially wisdom theology (see Proverbs 1:20-33).

Qoheleth discovers several reasons why the traditional ways do not lead to genuine insight into a meaningful existence. First, God has ordered and structured the creation in such a rigorous fashion that everything happens according to a preset plan. In fact, this orderly creation is so structured that persons, too, are intimate parts of the grand design, playing only the role assigned to them by God. They make no real contribution to the operations of a mechanistic world order. Our roles are minimal and are of little significance (1:13-14).

Second, all existence is vanity because God has chosen to conceal the divine purpose from the mind of humans (3:11). In other words, there is no revelation! Human beings know that God created the world, and that God made everything beautiful, but further insights into God's will and purpose remain hidden.

Finally, Qoheleth probes the traditional Hebrew belief in divine retribution—the notion that God distinguishes between the righteous and the wicked. But he concludes that such distinctions do not occur in real life (3:16). Qoheleth finds even the judicial system fraught with injustice; this is the ultimate irony. The traditional explanation that innocent suffering is only a test (3:18) fails Qoheleth's logic. And with no substantial life beyond death, persons' fates are the same as that of the beast—namely death. Both spirits go down to the earth. And divine retribution goes unfulfilled.

Qoheleth challenges traditional Hebrew faith on the basis of his human experience, and he concludes that wisdom theology has claimed more than it can verify. God and God's ways remain a mystery to this ancient sage, and human existence is not altogether a happy situation. But never once does Qoheleth deny or even doubt God's existence. Even with all the contradictions and perplexities of human existence, the reality of God remains beyond question. Not much can be known about God or God's purpose on earth, but God's existence cannot be questioned. The challenge of Qoheleth is directed at what persons have claimed about God rather than at God's existence.

§ § § § § § §

Ecclesiastes 4–8

Introduction to These Chapters

Ecclesiastes 4–8 may be divided into the following parts.

  I. Social Injustice (4:1-3)
 II. Better This Than That (4:4-16)
III. Miscellaneous Observations (5:1-20)
 IV. More Vanities on Earth (6:1-12)
  V. Wisdom and the Wise (7:1-29)
 VI. The Plight of Human Finitude (8:1-17)

Social Injustice (4:1-3)

In theme, 4:1-3 connects with 3:16-22 in complaining about social injustice. Qoheleth observes that the poor stand alone, with none to comfort them. This conclusion contrasts sharply with Proverbs, where many sayings attest to divine protection for the poor and the terrible consequences arising from mistreatment of the poor. (See Proverbs 19:17; 22:22-23.) Qoheleth finds no such help for them. In fact, even the child who has not yet been born is better off than the poor and the already deceased, since he or she has not yet seen the miseries of human existence. Qoheleth here contradicts his later conclusion that a living dog is better than a dead lion (9:4).

Better This Than That (4:4-16)

These verses contain Qoheleth's observation on different ethical situations and different motivations that inspire conduct. Regarding theme, there is little connection among the units in this section, except that they are random observations on a variety of unfortunate circumstances plaguing human beings in their existence on earth.

Verses 4, 5, and 6 form a brief unit describing the utter futility of work or industriousness. First (verse 4), Qoheleth observes that, in reality, jealousy is the primary motivation for all human effort. Persons, he implies, are not motivated by pride in their work, or by a sense of accomplishment, or even by a desire to use their talents wisely. Instead, persons are motivated by envy of other persons' possessions or their social or economic status.

Next, Qoheleth cites a traditional proverb (see Proverbs 19:15, 24; 28:19) advocating the disastrous consequences of laziness. A fool simply sits around, does nothing, and wastes away. He or she should be working, harvesting crops, using his or her energy wisely.

But, says Qoheleth, such energetic work itself is sheer folly (verse 6). For a life of ease is vastly superior to the life of an overachiever, or even a hard worker. After all, industriousness is merely chasing wind; it is futile! Clearly verse 6 contradicts verse 5, but this style of citing a traditional saying and then refuting it is characteristic of the author. Contradiction is a fact of human existence, for Qoheleth.

Part of the reason human effort is futile is that one may have no heirs (verses 7-8). With no one to inherit the fruits of one's labor, and since persons rarely enjoy the rewards of their own work, Qoheleth aptly asks, Why bother? (4:8).

In contrast to verse 8, Qoheleth affirms the advantages of strong social relationships—two are better than one (verse 9). Companions can aid each other in times of need and they are stronger together than individually, just as a thrice wrapped cord is stronger than a single strand.

The final theme in this chapter is the impermanence of

royal fame. Qoheleth contrasts a poor but wise youth with an aged but foolish king. Usually age brings respect and admiration to a ruler, but not here because the king is unwilling to heed counsel. No matter, Qoheleth reminds us, that this older king had arisen from humble beginnings to sit upon the throne. Soon he will be replaced by that wise, young lad. Memory of the king will soon fade. But in time, this lad, too, will be forgotten. Memories are short-lived, even for kings, young and old.

Miscellaneous Observations (5:1-20)

This chapter consists of four principal themes: (1) advice regarding religious conduct (verses 1-7); (2) advantages of a king (verses 8-9); (3) problems associated with wealth (verses 10-17); and (4) advice to enjoy life and accept one's lot (verses 18-20).

In the initial section (verses 1-7), Qoheleth urges great restraint and caution in performing religious obligations. Proper respect should characterize one's attitude toward God. Sacrifices should be made quietly and sincerely, otherwise not at all. Cautious speech should be used in the presence of God—fools chatter constantly and offend God (verse 3). Finally, one must exercise care in making vows to God, particularly vows that one might be unable to fulfill. Promises uttered before God are binding and must therefore be chosen with the greatest of care. Qoheleth then closes with a injunction to fear God (not a question as indicated in the NRSV).

At first, this judicious advice on matters of religion may appear out of place in Qoheleth's memoirs. After all, God and God's ways remain a total mystery to human beings (3:11). Some scholars earlier in this century felt this section was added later by a pious scribe who wanted to make Qoheleth's words less heretical. Actually, however, these instructions concur rather well with Qoheleth's ethics of moderation (7:16). In the absence of any evidence to the contrary, persons should honor tradition and observe carefully the rules of the religious cult. One never knows when the Lord might decide to look this way.

Religion seems to function in a utilitarian way for Qoheleth—it is useful in avoiding potential dangers. God's power is as incomprehensible as are God's ways and words. Respect (the fear of God) is always the best attitude, Qoheleth suggests. Such a practical attitude is certainly not out of character for Qoheleth.

In verses 8-9, Qoheleth notes the hierarchical structure of government, corrupted from top to bottom by greed for money or power. At the bottom the poor are victimized by unscrupulous overlords; they are overtaxed and undercompensated. But the overlord's mistreatment of the poor is being carefully observed (and possibly duplicated) by officials higher up, who themselves are corrupt, and so on up the line to the king. This is a sad commentary on the evils within the structure of Qoheleth's society. But this bureaucratic corruption notwithstanding, Qoheleth still feels that a king brings order and stability to an agrarian country.

Verses 10-17 indicate Qoheleth's negative judgments on wealth. In verse 10 Qoheleth observes, astutely, that persons motivated by the desire to accumulate wealth will never be satisfied. They will always want more, and even more—in a never-ending quest. This lack of any ultimate satisfaction or contentment gives rise to emptiness—vanity (*meaninglessness*).

His second observation is that wealth attracts many friends (see Proverbs 19:6-7). Everyone wants to associate with the rich and the famous—so much so that these leeches consume one's entire wealth. This leaves the rich with nothing, except the vision of their wealth disappearing. Wealth brings only disappointment and constant frustration.

Next, Qoheleth notes the peaceful rest that comes to

the laborer, while the wealthy person lies awake tossing and worrying (verse 12). The more wealth one has, the more one worries about how to protect what one has and how to increase one's economic worth.

Finally, Qoheleth describes the unfortunate situation of a wealthy man who lost his fortune in a "bad venture" and now has nothing left to bequeath to his son. His days of toil and hard work end with nothing to show except vexation, sickness, and resentment. His legacy to his son is earthly misery instead of a good inheritance.

Qoheleth closes chapter 5 with his positive proposal about what persons should do in the face of the oppressions in human existence—namely that they should eat, drink, and enjoy life. God, in mysterious wisdom, gives us wealth and possessions along with the power to enjoy these gifts. We should accept our lot, enjoy our labor, and make no attempt to comprehend the purpose of God. Enjoy life!

More Vanities on Earth (6:1-12)

In verses 1-6, Qoheleth presents a position opposite to his stand in 5:18-20. There, he describes the joy that comes to the person to whom God has given the power to enjoy wealth and possessions (5:19). But in 6:1-6, he describes the frustrations of those who lack the gift of enjoying the rewards of their labors. These unfortunate persons receive great wealth and honor—they lack nothing except the opportunity to enjoy them.

Even though these persons have countless children to carry forward their name, without being able to enjoy life's pleasures and without a proper burial even one with an *untimely birth* (NRSV; NIV = *a stillborn child*) is better off than they are. Ancient Israel attached great importance to a proper burial (see 1 Samuel 31:13), but exactly what significance Qoheleth associates with it is unclear. To be unable to enjoy life's few rewards is bad enough, but compounding one's misery by a miserly funeral only adds insult to injury. One frustration follows another.

Finally, the frustration at being unable to enjoy life's pleasures is intensified by the reality of a common fate—death! Such a situation, for Qoheleth, is truly an evil situation.

In verses 7-9, Qoheleth ponders the futility of human appetite and desires. He cites a traditional proverb stating that most persons are motivated to hard work as a means of satisfying their basic appetites (Proverbs 16:26). But in the end, the wise and wealthy person gains no real advantage over the foolish and poor person. They all have a common fate. With this reality in view, Qoheleth concludes that one does better in life to enjoy what is available immediately and refrain from wishful thinking or strong desires. These dreams can lead only to depression and frustration.

Qoheleth ends this chapter with some reflections on the limitations of human knowledge and meaningful participation in the created order. Just as the poem in chapter 3 describes the rigid determinism of the universe, Qoheleth reaffirms here that human beings cannot alter the pre-established course of existence. Neither can persons comprehend the purpose of this existence, regardless of how much they talk (verse 11). Human beings have no real knowledge of value during their brief sojourns on earth, nor do they have any substantial knowledge of the future. Limited in authentic contributions, unaware of moral values, and uncertain of the future, persons are totally consumed by the vanity of existence, says Qoheleth.

Wisdom and the Wise (7:1-29)

Verses 1-14 consist of miscellaneous sayings and observations from Qoheleth. Judging from the conventional theme of some sayings (7:1a, 7, 9, 11-12), Qoheleth has drawn from orthodox wisdom such as that found in Proverbs. To these conventional sayings, Qoheleth adds key words and phrases that reflect his basic scepticism. For example, verse 1a extols the value of a good reputation (see Proverbs 22:1). To this orthodox saying in 1a, Qoheleth adds a pessimistic clause in 1b expressing a preference for death (because the miseries are just beginning).

Verse 2: This comparative saying may easily have been penned in Qoheleth's own hand, since it expresses a preference for mourning rather than for feasting. When one realizes that life brings few joys, gross injustices, and no meaning, one weeps rather than rejoices.

Verse 3: A sober, realistic (albeit sorrowful) appraisal of human existence provides one with a greater sense of satisfaction than naive belief. This theme is similar to that of verses 1 and 2.

Verse 4: The wise person realizes the sad plight of human existence, while the fool celebrates in total ignorance. See also verses 1-3.

Verses 5-6: The honest corrections of a wise person are much more valuable than the mirth of fools. Just as a small amount of wood in a fire produces little heat, the deceptive laughter of fools leads nowhere and provides no rewards.

Verse 7: Bribery is particularly evil, since it corrodes the justice systems. (See also Proverbs 17:23.)

Verse 8: Since the end of a matter signals its completion, one has more to celebrate at that point than at the beginning. A calm disposition is much more desirable than a hot temper (see Proverbs 16:32). These sayings are doubtless from the collections of orthodox wisdom teaching.

Verse 9: See verse 8b. See also Proverbs 22:24-25.

Verse 10: Since history essentially repeats itself (1:3-11), the wise person is acutely aware that the former days were not really better than the present times.

Nothing changes! Life was oppressive then, just as it is now.

Verses 11-12: While wisdom may not enable a person to understand completely the mysteries of creation or to comprehend the purpose of human existence, it does, nevertheless, have some practical benefits. Stated briefly, wisdom enables one to live more comfortably and more securely.

Verses 13-14: Qoheleth observes that God predetermined matters so that human beings cannot alter the plan. If good fortune befalls a person, he or she should rejoice. But if evil should occur, he or she should remember that God also arranged this. One never knows the future. Accept what happens as being what should happen.

Verses 15-22: These verses contain Qoheleth's consideration of moderation as normative in ethical behavior. Even in the absence of infallible divine retribution (verse 15), one should nevertheless exercise some respect for moral virtue, but not to an extreme. Neither should excessive wickedness lead one to an early grave. Instead of either of these extremes, a moderate position, coupled with due respect for God, can lead to a better life. Even religion, for Qoheleth, serves a very utilitarian purpose.

Wisdom (as in verses 11-12) has some practical benefits, and a wise person probably has more advantages than ten rulers. But wisdom does not guarantee absolute moral perfection (verse 20). After all, no one is so righteous that he or she does not occasionally fall victim to vice. Just as servants may curse their masters, everyone must remember that they have occasionally said similar things about other persons.

The real point Qoheleth makes in this section is that absolute human moral perfection is impossible, and retribution does not always occur as it should. Accordingly, one should adopt moderation and tolerance as ethical norms, while concurrently observing due respect for God's order.

Verses 23-29: Qoheleth closes this chapter with a report on his test to discover meaning by way of wisdom. But, as in 1:13 and 2:12, he concludes that such matters are far beyond his grasp. He then reports turning his attention to more practical matters such as morality and immorality. Few men, he observes, and almost no women, exercise real virtue. Some women, in fact, snare unsuspecting men in their webs of wickedness. Somehow, the entire human race has slipped from its earlier created state of virtue, and now continues immoral living, intentionally or unintentionally.

The Plight of Human Finitude (8:1-17)

Since verse 1 has the wise man as its subject, it is probably related best to 7:23-29. There Qoheleth expresses his low estimate of humanity in general. But in 8:1 he concludes that there may be a few men whose wisdom make a visible difference. The glowing face and changed countenance are clear evidence of superior wisdom and inward character. Unfortunately Qoheleth does not identify either the nature or source of this wisdom, and he certainly limits it to a few wise men, as suggested by the two rhetorical questions at the beginning (8:1).

In keeping with his practical approach to morality and virtuous living, Qoheleth urges persons to exercise great care in their behavior before kings. For better or for worse, kings wield tremendous power over citizens' lives. Whenever one makes a promise to (or before) the king, the promise must be fulfilled, even if the matter is unpleasant. One should avoid questioning the king about a decision, for his word is sovereign. When the king issues a command, it should be obeyed quickly and without question. Matters have all been predetermined, and the structures of existence must be maintained—the king is part of this prearranged structure.

Since death is the eventual end, and not knowing what is really going on in human existence, one is prudent to obey the commands of the king. There is no escape from the structure of existence, including death. Even within this rigid, prearranged order for existence some persons cruelly inflict needless suffering on their fellows.

In verses 10-15, Qoheleth returns to the theme of divine retribution with which he has struggled earlier (3:16-22). As in the previous section, Qoheleth laments the vanity that wicked persons often fail to receive their just punishment. Instead, much to his utter dismay, the wicked receive wide public acclaim and are given elaborate funerals. This situation is truly vain and gives occasion to question divine justice.

Yet, Qoheleth's traditional wisdom faith assures him that the evildoer will not go unpunished (verses 12-13). This disparity between Qoheleth's experiences in real life and his traditional faith constitutes an irreconcilable tension. Intellectual honesty requires that Qoheleth face up to his real-life experience. His faith demands trust in divine justice. Yet these two elements contradict one another, and cause serious doubts.

This contradiction, in part, leads Qoheleth to conclude that *all is vanity* (*meaningless*). In the face of this state of affairs, Qoheleth counsels enjoyment of life as it comes.

The chapter ends with Qoheleth's scepticism regarding humankind's ultimate knowledge of God's intentions. Since he stated this conclusion earlier (3:10-11), verses 16-17 add no new dimension to the book. Human beings are unable to discern any sort of divine purpose or divine plan. Not even the wise person has such insight, even though he or she claims to know the ways of God.

§ § § § § § §

The Message of Ecclesiastes 4–8

Qoheleth concludes that not even wisdom can enable persons to discover God's scheme of things on earth. In 7:24, he laments that such ultimate meaning is *far off, and very deep* (NRSV; NIV = *most profound*). In 8:17, he observes that regardless of how much one works at it, one cannot discover God's work. Persons must learn to live without any real sense of meaning, purpose, or value—at least not as the sages in Proverbs claimed could be known. So, Qoheleth asks, what is good for one to do, faced with this limited knowledge? Give up and die? Certainly not! What Qoheleth recommends is practical morality, centering in these chapters around five behaviors: (1) enjoying companionship of friends (4:9-12); (2) paying proper attention to religious observances, including the vows one makes before God (5:1-7); (3) maintaining moderation in all things (7:15-18); (4) respecting the authority and power of the king (8:2-9); and (5) enjoying life, including one's toil, for that is God's gift (8:15).

Although there are no absolute guarantees that these behaviors will result in happiness and prosperity, they do enable most persons to endure an otherwise meaningless and oppressive existence. Life offers few rewards, so one should take advantage of the few benefits available, such as friendship, good food, good drink, and whatever wealth one may acquire. For even as perplexing as life is, it is still much better than death.

§ § § § § § §

Introduction to These Chapters

Chapters 9–12 may be outlined as follows.
I. One Fate Comes to All (9:1-3)
II. Life Is Superior to Death (9:4-10)
III. Time and Chance (9:11-12)
IV. Wisdom's Limited Value (9:13-18)
V. Miscellaneous Sayings (10:1-20)
VI. Further Sayings (11:1-6)
VII. The Joys of Youth (11:7-10)
VIII. A Parting Word (12:1-8)
IX. Later Additions (12:9-14)

One Fate Comes to All (9:1-3)

Continuing the theme of limited human knowledge
(8:17), Qoheleth analyzes retribution in light of the *same
fate* (NRSV; NIV = *common destiny*). Human beings live in
a state of darkness with regard to God's ways and
purposes. Persons simply do not know God's attitude
toward them, whether it is love or hate. About the only
certainty in life is death; but death comes to everyone
alike, to the righteous and to the evil, to the clean and to
the unclean, to one who observes religious obligations
faithfully and to one who ignores them.

With a common fate that erases all distinctions among
persons, divine retribution is difficult to affirm.
Certainly, Qoheleth cannot verify that God makes such
distinctions here on earth, rewarding the righteous and
punishing the wicked, for he knows from his own

experience that this is not so. Most persons, he says, are full of evil and *madness is in their hearts* (verse 3). Such a dismal picture of finite existence robs life of much of its beauty and grandeur. To live with the uncertainty of God's attitude toward human beings is truly to live on the precipice of absurdity. Nudging persons even closer to the edge is the reality that one fate comes to all persons.

Life Is Superior to Death (9:4-10)

Yet, even amid the anxieties and inequities of finite existence, Qoheleth affirms that life is superior to death (verse 4). Limited knowledge is better than no knowledge at all, and experiencing even the broad extremes of emotions (love-hate), is better than feeling no emotions whatever. At least with the living there is still the possibility of relative joys, but when one dies, any hope whatever perishes. With these limits in mind, Qoheleth offers three moral instructions for the living:

(1) Enjoy life with food and drink; God has prearranged everything (verse 7).

(2) Observe proper moral and religious regulations (verse 8).

(3) Enjoy the companionship of your mate, work hard at your labor, and enjoy whatever blessings may come your way (verses 9-10).

These practical values may be far from the grandiose gifts promised by wisdom (see Proverbs 1:20-33). But they do offer limited possibilities for coping with human existence without desiring death. Sheol's (death's) rewards are even less attractive than life among the living. Qoheleth resolutely believes that persons can find life enjoyable, even with limited knowledge, with no retribution and with a common fate.

Time and Chance (9:11-12)

Verses 11-12 restate Qoheleth's earlier conclusion that there is no divine retribution on earth (see the comments on 3:16-22). Since persons do not understand the ways of God, they do not know the nature and limits of their own times (verse 12). This perception makes human existence seem arbitrary or appear to operate by chance. But this is not the case at all (see 3:1-11). Rather, our limited knowledge means that persons are not privy to God's plans and do not know God's timetable. Therefore, we are all hapless victims of what seem to be operations of time and chance (verse 11). In reality, we are all part of God's prearranged plan.

Wisdom's Limited Value (9:13-18)

In verses 13-18, Qoheleth describes the limited and temporary values of wisdom. He cites the example of the poor wise man whose wisdom delivered an entire city, but yet was not remembered by the residents of the city. Even though the poor wise man's words could have been ignored, or even hated, they are still more valuable than brute strength. This limited value, however, can be easily offset by a single evildoer (verse 18). A small amount of evil outweighs a large amount of wisdom.

Miscellaneous Sayings (10:1-20)

Verse 1: This saying continues the thought expressed in 9:18b—*but one sinner* (NIV; NRSV = *bungler*) *destroys much good.* The tantalizing aroma of perfume can be tainted by the stench of dead flies. Similarly, it takes only a little folly to counteract much wisdom and honor.

Verse 2: The *heart* is the source of moral goodness for the sage; it is one's inner self or soul. Generally, the sage envisions the right side as morally right and the left as morally wrong. The wise person has some moral insight whereas the fool lacks knowledge altogether. This thought continues Qoheleth's limited endorsement of wisdom (see 9:13-18).

Verse 3: The folly of the fool is self-evident—all can

clearly see it for themselves. Again, Qoheleth offers a nod in support of orthodox wisdom.

Verse 4: If one angers the king, the best response is to remain calm, appease him if possible, and allow his anger to abate. This advice represents the practical nature of Qoheleth's ethics. Actually his advice is really no different in this matter from what the orthodox counsel of a sage would be.

Verses 5-7: Qoheleth observes inversions (or perversions) within the social order: errors made by the king, fools with great power, slaves on horses, and princes on foot. Such radical inversions are inherently evil and cause much harm to the orderliness of society.

Verse 8: This saying is similar in theme to Proverbs 1:8-9; 26:27—evildoers often fall victim to their own wicked traps. The robber often finds a surprise waiting inside the victim's house. In some situations, the law of act-consequence operates well.

Verse 9: Different occupations entail different dangers.

Verse 10: Wisdom provides an edge or advantage in life, just as a sharpened ax cuts better than a dull ax does.

Verse 11: Once the snake has bitten a person, the snake-charmer is unnecessary. There is a proper sequence for all matters, including ways of avoiding dangerous snakebites.

Verses 12-15: This sub-collection of sayings characterizes the deleterious behavior of fools; their talk causes them nothing but misery. Fools ramble on aimlessly, talking about matters about which no one knows anything. They are gregarious and lazy.

Verses 16-20: Verses 16, 17, and 20 are sayings about the king. In verse 16, a land mourns for the lack of strong, forceful leadership because its king is merely a lad and the princes are wasting their time in gluttony. By contrast, the land rejoices (verse 17) when its king reigns supreme and the princes celebrate properly.

In verse 20, persons are urged to be cautious and

discreet with their criticism of powerful persons such as the king or the rich; such comments could get back to them, causing their anger and vindictiveness to do harm to their critics. Verse 18 condemns laziness and verse 19 celebrates the economic benefits of industry. Indolence allows one's house to collapse, while the wealth that comes from hard work solves many problems. Most sayings in this chapter reflect conventional wisdom, rather than Qoheleth's scepticism. More important, they support practical conclusions drawn from experience. In this chapter, Qoheleth's tradition as a sage comes together with his real-life experience. Earlier, in chapters 1 and 2, his tradition and his experience conflicted. But here, Qoheleth is able to affirm a limited value to wisdom, and to propose at least some ethical values—even if these values are temporary and relative. He is not an ethical nihilist.

Further Sayings (11:1-6)

Verse 1: This admonition is difficult to interpret, as suggested by the numerous meanings assigned to it by various scholars. Qoheleth recommends taking risks with one's capital in expectation of great rewards. In other words, "nothing ventured, nothing gained." Since life is filled with uncertainties, why not take a chance?

Verse 2: This verse is not a recommendation for charity. Rather, Qoheleth commends diversifying one's economic resources—spreading out one's investments in view of life's uncertainties.

Verse 3: Qoheleth here repeats his earlier conclusion that the laws of nature are predetermined by God and cannot be altered. One should proceed as best one can with one's life, not knowing what lies ahead.

Verse 4: This is a sarcastic comment on laziness. See Proverbs 26:13-15; Ecclesiastes 10:18. Staring at the clouds never produces anything of substance.

Verse 5: Qoheleth draws attention again to the limited scope of human knowledge (see also 3:16; 8:16). Again, he implies that incomplete knowledge of God's plans must not lead one to complete inactivity. We should proceed as best we can to achieve as much as we can.

Verse 6: This saying makes essentially the same point as verse 5—one must proceed with life's activities despite the uncertainties of human existence.

The Joys of Youth (11:7-10)

With verse 7 Qoheleth begins to bring his memoirs to a conclusion. Despite all of life's uncertainties, all of its predetermined rigidity, all of its unfairness and mysteries, Qoheleth still believes that life is preferable to death (see also 9:4-5). In a much more elegant style here, he reaffirms the intrinsic value and beauty of life itself—it is pleasant merely to view the sun (verse 7). Qoheleth basks in the sunlight; he warms himself in the rays of opportunity; he absorbs all that life offers. For he knows that vanity and darkness lie ahead, somewhere (verse 8).

Qoheleth revels in the celebration of youth, urging his younger readers to appreciate their present days of splendor. He tells them to follow their hearts and satisfy the visions of their eyes, while being ever-mindful that God will hold them accountable. The days of youth should be enjoyed, because such time passes quickly and the road that lies ahead is dismal and dark. But for the days of youth, pleasures abound in great number.

A Parting Word (12:1-8)

This beautiful and well-known poem describes in almost incomparable words the onset of old age and the problems it brings. Even while persons are young, they must be mindful of their accountability to God, and of the impending assault of age. For aging brings further woes, making an already burdensome life even more difficult. Old age robs persons of any joy in celebrating the advent of a new day, or the majesty of moonlight and starlight. The sense of cleanness and newness that ordinarily follows the rain now turns sour and dark, and one experiences only the return of clouds after clouds. Even once-mighty men bow with advent of old age (verse 3). The teeth fail to work. The eyes cannot see as well as once they saw. One cannot hear as sharply as one once heard (verse 4). A sense of fear and panic haunts the aged. The hair turns white and the body grows fat. Persons lose their sexual powers (verse 5). Death comes quickly (verse 6), with the dissolution of the body, which returns to the dust, and the return of the spirit to God.

In verse 8, Qoheleth concludes his book exactly as he began: *Vanity of vanities . . . all is vanity* (NRSV; NIV = *meaningless, meaningless. Everything is meaningless*). He has completed his memoirs, shared his doubts, and put life into its proper perspective. And still, all is vanity.

Later Additions (12:9-14)

These final additions seem to close the book with a positive, appreciative word. Perhaps this later editor also supplied the superscription at the beginning (1:1). He identifies Qoheleth as a sage who spent much time composing and arranging sayings. He praises Qoheleth's effort to find the right words with which to speak the truth.

In verse 11, the final addition indicates the seriousness with which he holds Qoheleth's words; they are set, and nothing is to be added or deleted. Many books have been written, but too much study makes one weary—as it did Qoheleth.

Finally, as if to offset some of Qoheleth's scepticism, the editor adds his praise and benediction that affirm faith and reassert his belief in divine retribution.

§ § § § § § §

The Message of Ecclesiastes 9–12

After considerable thought, carefully weighing his experience and his tradition, Qoheleth concludes that persons know very little about God's will or God's ways (8:16–9:2). He has no confidence in reason's perception of the created order, including divine retribution (9:2-3). While God has prearranged nature so that we have seasons and times, one cannot be certain what they are or of what lies ahead. This pervasive scepticism leaves Qoheleth insecure about exactly what and how much persons can know about the operations of the world.

This scepticism would paralyze some persons, as far as any real activity is concerned. But not Qoheleth. Although life is replete with uncertainties, and granted that our knowledge is very limited, Qoheleth urges us to go ahead with life, enjoy what pleasures we can (9:7-9), be venturesome in our commercial activities (11:1), diversify our economic interests (11:2), and enjoy our youthful days.

We never know what sort of rewards may come our way. Life still offers much more than death offers. To act decisively in the face of existential uncertainty is to display courage and deep resolve. To act without certainty that clear and knowable consequences will result is to forego human weakness. To live under the cloud of divine mystery is to live alone and in isolation from God. But at least it is to live rather than to die.

§ § § § § § §

Introduction to Song of Solomon

From A.D. 90 at the Council of Jamnia, where Jewish rabbis met to establish the Hebrew canon, the Song of Solomon has evoked the broadest range of human reaction. At Jamnia, Rabbi Akiba is reported to have called this little book the Holy of Holies, referring to its special place in Hebrew life. Some Christians revered it as an allegory about Christ and his love for the church, while other Christians reacted negatively to its sensual, erotic imagery.

Other students of the Bible, both Jewish and Christian, condemned the book for the lack of a single reference to God in any verse. Yet others prized the work for its profound insight into love and human physical attraction. Imaginations have been taxed beyond their limits in an effort to identify the lovers and to untangle the seemingly disjointed sequence of love songs. But even with all of its mystery and ambiguities, Song of Solomon was included in the canon. Today, it presents one of the most eloquent and moving tributes to love in all of literature.

The Name of the Book

In the Hebrew Bible, the book is entitled Song of Songs, and forms, along with four other shorter books, a group known as the *Five Megilloth* (scrolls). These five books are read during the Jewish celebration of Passover. In the English translations of the Bible, the book is called *Song of Solomon*, whereas in Roman Catholic versions it is called *Canticles*. The name derived from the first words in the Hebrew text is literally *song of all songs*.

The Date of the Writing

A specific date for Song of Solomon is difficult to determine, because there are few reliable historical references in the book and because the songs seem to reflect more than a single author. Solomon's name appears six times in the book: 1:5; 3:7, 9, 11; 8:11-12. Most of the instances suggest Solomon's fame or his reputation as a singer. Or they even identify him as the *beloved*, but do not actually identify him as the author.

Elsewhere, Tirzah, the tenth-century capital of the Northern Kingdom, is mentioned in parallelism to Jerusalem (6:4). Perhaps, however, the most important evidence for dating the material is the appearance of foreign terms, such as a Persian word for *garden* in 4:12 and a Greek word, *palanquin*, in 3:9. Many words and syntactical elements in Song of Solomon are unique in the Old Testament. In view of all these factors, most scholars cautiously assign a date for final composition to the fourth or third century B.C. This date allows for several songs that may date much earlier, possibly as far back as the tenth or ninth century, as suggested by the Tirzah-Jerusalem parallel.

The Author of the Book

Likewise, it is difficult to identify the author of Song of Solomon. The superscription (1:1) ascribes these songs to Solomon; however, the Hebrew preposition used, taken by some scholars as indicating authorship, may actually have several other meanings: for Solomon, to Solomon, or about Solomon. Clearly, as the patron sage of wisdom in Israel, Solomon is the honoree, and is probably the pseudonymous lover and bridegroom. After all, the author of 1 Kings 4:32 refers to King Solomon as the composer of over one thousand songs. Finally, the book's inclusion in the Hebrew canon is generally attributed to its association with Solomon, although other reasons probably contributed also.

The book has the literary nature of an anthology rather than a continuous poetic narrative or hymn. There are too many logical inconsistencies, contradictions, and repetitions for the book to be from a single hand. So, although it is unlikely that Solomon could have written the entire book, he is doubtless the central figure and the recipient of the amorous affection of the heroine.

Interpretations of the Book

Due to the numerous literary and thematic complications in Song of Solomon, interpretations have been many and diverse. Basically, these different interpretations may be divided into five groups: allegorical, cultic, dramatic, liturgical, and secular.

The allegorical interpretation flourished among many Jews and early Christians, but has few adherents today. The rabbis saw the book as an expression of the intimate covenant relationship between God and Israel (see also Genesis 15; Jeremiah 31:31-34). Drawing on the motif of human marriage as symbolizing these covenants, early rabbis saw in Song of Solomon many images that had been developed by prophets such as Hosea and Jeremiah. Later, Christians such as Origen and Augustine saw the book as an allegory of Christ and his bride, the church. These multi-level interpretations disregarded the human aspect of love, opting instead to symbolize the entire book as meaningful only on another, more spiritual level.

The second major school of interpretation is the cultic school. According to these scholars, Song of Solomon is an adaptation of a pagan religious rite centering on the mythological dying/rising god motif, as found in Greece and Egypt. Still other scholars suggest that the book arose from the rituals found in early Canaanite nature/fertility myths. The sexual imagery in both (or either) liturgies celebrates a seasonal renewal of life, and depicts the eager anticipation of the maiden for her lover's return. The springtime setting, the theme of the absentee-lover, and the dancing rites (6:13) all support this interpretation.

A third interpretation relates Song of Solomon to certain Greek tragedies. Some scholars identify two characters while other scholars find three roles—a king, his beloved, and a shepherd. A chorus serves as background. Some type of plot emerges that pits the king against a shepherd lad for the affections of a young maiden. The drama is incomplete because the dramatic struggle has been left out of the present book.

A fourth view sees Song of Solomon as a series of Judean wedding songs, similar to certain songs and marriage celebrations among Syrian peasants. The bride and groom assume the identities of king and queen and celebrate the beauty of their physical natures in preparation for their wedding.

Finally, the book may be seen as a collection of secular love poetry, celebrating the eternal bliss of physical love. There is no hint of immorality here, no lusting, no eroticisms, and no adultery. Instead, what we find is a moving testimony to that fundamental passion that moves the very souls of men and women, drawing them together in a moment of sheer passion. Such a strong physical attraction lies at the heart of any loving relationship. But marriage is the context for this celebration, eliminating adultery or promiscuity as the setting.

The Content of the Book
These songs have been collected and edited much as an anthology. Many of them reflect a rural or pastoral setting; still other songs display signs of cult and ritual.

Together, they form an anthology of love songs and love poems that affirm the pure goodness of physical passion.

Absent from Song of Solomon are the great theological traditions in the Old Testament, such as the covenants with Abraham, with Moses, and with David. There is not a single reference to the Exodus, to the law, or to divine revelation. In fact, there is no mention of God at all. Retribution (or the absence thereof) occupies not a single line. Instead, we have in this book an affirmation of the uninhibited joy of physical love between a man and a woman. This is nature at its best—unashamed, undefiled, and uncorrupted by society's norms.

Song of Solomon 1-4

Introduction to These Chapters

These chapters may be outlined as follows.

Superscription (1:1)

The Hebrew phrase *Song of Songs* is a superlative,
similar in form to *Holy of Holies*. The phrase suggests that
these songs are among the most beautiful of all songs.
The relative pronoun *which* appears in this verse in a
longer grammatical form than elsewhere in the book,
where it appears only as a particle. This shift in form
suggests that, as is the case with many other books, the
superscription is a secondary addition. As indicated in
the Introduction, the ambiguity of the Hebrew pronoun

relating the work to Solomon indicates honor or dedication at least as much as it means authorship.

Come Let Us Love (1:2-4)

This promising introduction (1:2), spoken by the maiden, eagerly invites the kisses and other affections of her lover, the king. She encourages him with enticements of flattery: *your love is better (more delightful) than wine,* and so forth. She compares him to the value of precious oil (possibly ointments). She is overwhelmed by a sense of urgency, until finally her wish is fulfilled and she finds herself nestled in her lover's arms when he has brought her into his chamber.

Then, a chorus reaffirms the maiden's amorous intentions. Her love for her king, her lover, is sanctioned in the purity of her intent as well as in the sincerity of her feelings.

This interpretation favors the view that Song of Solomon is a collection of secular love songs. The speakers are a maiden (deeply in love), her lover, the king, and a chorus. The allegorical interpretation would make the speaker Israel, the bride of Yahweh, or the church, the bride of Christ. The liturgical view would see the speakers as the bride beginning a lavish marriage ceremony. The cultic interpretation would have the speaker as a mythical goddess in pursuit of her lost love. While each of these interpretations has much to commend it, the book is most likely a collection of love poems, used in various marriage and/or cultic ceremonies.

Thus the first song rejoices in the invitation of the maiden to her lover, the king, and his acceptance of her love. There is no hint here of shame or guilt at her free and open expression of natural love between a man and woman. In fact, the rabbis included this book precisely because it does celebrate the wondrous miracle of human love, including affection and sexual attraction. Pure love is not a moral aberration.

The Maiden's Vineyards (1:5-6)

Here the maiden speaks of her elegant, dark complexion, derived from hours spent tending her family's vineyard. She compares the beauty of her skin to the dark goat-hair tents of desert bedouins, and to the splendor of the curtains in Solomon's royal palace. Although she worked under duress in the family vineyards out-of-doors, her own vineyard she has freely given to her lover. Her brother's anger, in reality, made her only more beautiful with her tanned, healthy appearance.

The Maiden Searches for Her Lover (1:7-8)

One of the standard themes in great love stories is the almost frantic search for the absent lover. Here, too, the maiden seeks her lost lover. The pastoral allusions here suggest that her lover is a shepherd rather than a king, as in 4a. The alternation between shepherd and king may suggest that either we have separate songs or the lover assumes different roles as the play develops in order to heighten the dramatic effect. Given the different vocabularies and styles that exist in Song of Solomon, the first suggestion is more plausible.

The maiden seeks her beloved shepherd in order to be with him as he pastures his flocks. Just as his flocks need his attention, the maiden desires his affection. Indeed, she is more than merely one of many persons who follow behind his flock—she is his beloved.

The chorus responds in verse 8 by telling the maiden to follow the trails of the shepherds, pasturing her own flocks in places where they have been. She is certain to find him there.

An Analogy of Beauty (1:9-11)

For the first time, the king, her lover, speaks. In a simple but elegant analogy, he compares his beloved maiden to a majestic, regal steed, prancing before an

Egyptian chariot. Horses were creatures of great beauty and worth, and when they were arrayed in the splendor of parade dress, they were exceptionally beautiful. Similarly, the maiden is to be dressed and bejeweled with ornaments of fine metals and precious stones, making her truly a vision of beauty.

The imagery here, as elsewhere, is figurative and evocative. The speaker is communicating his feelings rather than offering factual details. Thus to press the analogies too far is to misinterpret the text.

The Appeal of Her Lover (1:12-14)

Here, the maiden openly proclaims her powerful attraction to her king-lover, due to his aromatic fragrances. As they lie on his couch, she is overcome with desire. *Nard* (*perfume*), *myrrh*, and *henna* are all special fragrances that were believed to be aphrodisiacs.

En-gedi is a particularly beautiful oasis, lying just west of the southern shores of the Dead Sea. Its water brings refreshment to all who pause to drink, and furnishes a haven for lush vegetation.

An Exchange of Endearments (1:15-17)

The chapter ends with an exchange of endearments between the lover and her beloved. He proclaims the beauty of her eyes to be like that of doves (verse 15). She responds by acknowledging his beauty to be *truly lovely* (NRSV; NIV = *how charming*) (verse 16). She describes their home and its luxurious decor. This is truly a perfect love, housed in an elegant setting. They are a fitting couple because their personal qualities meld into a mutually beneficial relationship—exactly as God intended love to be.

The Maiden as a Flower (2:1-2)

The maiden identifies herself as a particular flower that thrives along the northern coastal plain in Israel,

Sharon. This plain is located just south of Mount Carmel and is lush and fertile. The *rose* or lily is indigenous to that region.

In verse 2, her beloved responds by complimenting his fair maiden as a *lily among brambles* (NRSV; NIV = *thorns*). His beautiful young companion is a woman of exceptional attractiveness who walks tall among her peers.

The Lover's Wish (2:3-7)

As if returning the compliment (verse 2), the maiden compares her beloved to a stately apple tree, which produces its fruit, unique among the trees of the forest. Like the apple tree, her beloved is distinctive; he is truly one of a kind. She continues by describing a meeting with her lover in a *festive setting*.

Wrapped in love (verse 4) and feasting on sumptuous and erotic delicacies (verse 5), the young maiden confesses that she is completely enthralled in the moment of encounter. She dreams of his tender embrace and longs for his gentle touch (verse 6). Admonishing her attendants (the *daughters of Jerusalem*) by invoking sacred animals (*gazelles* and *does*), she requests privacy until their lovemaking has been completed (verse 7).

Many scholars find this section replete with imagery from fertility rites in ancient Semitic cultures. *Raisins* (see also Hosea 3:1) are especially suggestive of Canaanite cults. However, the vocabulary and sense of the entire section may equally well suggest an impending sexual encounter between two lovers. She requests aphrodisiacs in verse 5, dreams of their lovemaking in verse 6, and pleads for privacy until completion in verse 7.

A Visit from Her Lover (2:8-17)

The following scene is one of the most sensual experiences described in the entire book. The scene opens with a graphic account of the lover leaping and bounding over mountains and hills to celebrate the new birth of spring with his beloved maiden (verse 8). She describes his speed (*gazelle*) and his sexual powers (*stag*) with vivid images drawn from the order of animals. Peering inside from just beyond a wall that surrounds her house, her lover gazes inward through lattices that punctuate the wall. With a note of ecstatic joy, her lover announces the arrival of spring, when the earth replenishes her verdant domain. Winter has come and gone, and the rains have fertilized the whole of nature. All around signs of life emanate from below and stand erect (verse 13).

Then, the lover entices his beloved to come and go away with him to welcome the renewal of seasons. He refers to her as a *dove* (verse 14) who soars openly to the recesses of nature, and yet is demure and discreet. He pleads with her to allow him to gaze upon her beauty (verse 14) and to help him banish all hindrances to an immediate fulfillment of their desires (verse 15). For their time has arrived, their vineyards are in blossom (verse 15).

She responds lovingly by admitting him into her chamber where they prepare to consummate their love. To pasture his flock among the lilies refers to their lovemaking, which lasts far into the night. *Turn*, she says, inviting him to love her deeply and with great passion. The lady is unafraid to express her eagerness for involvement and her zeal meets responsive arms.

The beauty of blossoming spring is matched by the consuming passion of love fulfilled. No hint of guilt or shame darkens this union! The beauty of their love knows nothing of perversions or sexual misconduct. They feel a sense of trust and respect that inspires passion and warmth.

A Lost Lover Is Found (3:1-5)

The widely-used mythological theme of a lost lover surfaces here for the first time. Whether in cultic rites of dying-rising gods, or in a liturgical parting of bride and bridegroom, the two lovers are separated. A frantic search in the middle of a darkened night ensues. At last she discovers her missing lover, and they are reunited. Then the maiden admonishes her attendants not to disturb them until dawn, when their passions are fulfilled (see 2:7).

This section evokes deep pathos within the readers, not so much for the lost lover as for his distraught beloved. Her feelings of panic as she frantically searches the city streets at night elicit considerable empathy on our part. We can almost feel her sense of desperation, the gnawing fear inside her body. Apart from her lover, her soul gasps for breath, even unto death. Not even the watchmen who patrol the city at night can help her. At last she finds her lover, and they are together again. Her joy at finding him safe soars to even greater heights than before. Returning to her chamber, they seal their reunion, undisturbed by friend or foe.

A Royal Wedding (3:6-11)

In preparation for his wedding, the lover-groom assumes the role of King Solomon, assembles an impressive entourage, and processes forth ceremoniously to celebrate the festive day. Emerging from the rustic wilderness, the groom and his attendants march toward Jerusalem, stirring up dust (columns of smoke) and emitting scents of fragrance. The groom rides in a special *palanquin (carriage)* surrounded by a host of groomsmen dressed as a military honor-guard. The entire procession is met by the daughters of Zion who welcome the groom and his escorts into the royal city of David.

The assumption of a royal fiction prior to a wedding was customary in ancient Semitic cultures. To sanction the day as truly auspicious, the nuptial couple adorned themselves in their finest clothes and paraded through the streets as royalty entering into the Temple. Such a marriage tradition clearly stands behind this poem in

3:6-11. While a marriage custom clearly forms the social matrix for this particular song, it is doubtful that the entire book derives from this setting. There are other passages which strongly suggest other settings originally less ceremonial in nature (2:3-7). Some songs are simply love poems, with no particular setting other than human relationships.

The Beauty of the Maiden (4:1-7)

Similar descriptions of the beautiful maiden can be found also in 6:4-10 and 7:1-9. Highly nuanced words and dreams convey the image of an exquisite woman, distinguished by great physical beauty. The comparisons are intended to evoke images rather than to explain actual similarities. Also, we must remember that standards of beauty for ancient Israel may differ from our own modern taste. The entire section exudes a feeling of great admiration for this young woman. His descriptions of her may easily touch a note of understanding in each of us.

As for his description of his lady, he compares her eyes to those of a dove—bright and clear. Her hair is smooth and black, silky and healthy. Her smiles disclose a set of white teeth, clear like that of sheep about to be shorn. Her mouth is thin but red in color, delicate and sensitive. Her cheeks are ruddy and tan, full and firm. The neck of his beloved is stately and tall, displaying extraordinary dignity and poise. Her breasts are delicate and light. In sum, he concludes, she is perfect, with *no flaw*.

The Lover Rejoices in His Garden (4:8–5:1)

Following his alluring description of the maiden's exquisite beauty, the king-lover invites his beloved to leave her home, high atop an austere mountain, and join him in a rendezvous of love (4:8). The mountains of Lebanon lie to the immediate north of Israel, and are renowned for their snowcapped peaks and as centers for

Canaanite religious sanctuaries. Mount Hermon, called also by its Amorite name, Senir, was well-known during the early days of Israelite history as the abode of a Canaanite love goddess. Wild animals and treacherous terrain serve to warn all intruders of imminent danger.

Then, the lover describes the overwhelming effect the young maiden has exerted on him. She has literally ravished him or stolen his heart with amorous attraction. The expression *my sister* is to be taken euphemistically, not genetically, as suggested by similar expressions in Egyptian love poetry. She is the best of the best— attractive, loving, fragrant, and sweet of kiss. Her physical inducements are irresistible.

He next compares her to a garden, surrounded by high walls and a locked gate. This image is particularly appropriate since ancient oriental gardens were (and are presently) sites of great beauty and repose. They luxuriate in verdant splendor, even amid arid climates. Clear, the reference is to his maiden's chastity. She reserves all the beauty of her garden for her lover. Her garden is filled with choicest fruits, fragrant herbs, and tantalizing spices all fed by a fountain overflowing with life-giving water.

In verse 16, the maiden responds by inviting her lover to visit her garden and partake of her fruits. She commands the winds to distribute her fragrance far and wide, enticing her lover to be her garden-guest.

In 5:1, the lover responds—he comes to the garden of his beloved to enjoy her *fruits* (see 4:16). At last, the union between the two lovers is about to be consummated. The marriage ceremony ends and the wedded couple retire to their chambers. A chorus concludes by admonishing them to eat and drink deeply of their love. The anticipation has ended: Lovemaking is at hand.

§ § § § § § §

The Message of Song of Solomon 1– 4

The central theme in Song of Solomon is love—romantic love between a man and woman who unite in marriage. Quite possibly, selections from this book were used originally as parts of marriage rites, or were ritual texts in a religious ceremony. Whatever their original settings in life, they have been collected into a larger book and now form a lyrical celebration of human love. Ancient Near Eastern literature abounds with love poetry from all walks of life; in fact, Syrian love songs such as these punctuate many phases of rural life including courtship and marriage.

From the outset, this book is replete with the celebration of strong physical attraction. The sexual imagery in Song of Solomon is too obvious to be overlooked. References to actual lovemaking (2:6; 8:3) leave no doubt that the marriage is (or is about to be) consummated. There are other allusions to sexual activity, such as pasturing flocks (6:2), eating fruit (4:16), and so forth. The imagery of the latch, the bolt, and a head wet with dew (5:2-6) are vivid and clear. Yet, this material is not sensual or erotic in the negative, immoral sense of those terms. Instead, readers are offered the open and unashamed expression of sheer delight in the physical aspects of love.

When the king-lover offers his impression of his beloved's physical body, one does not recoil or cringe. The reader knows that there is nobleness in such affirmations. Nature has endowed men and women with bodies, with sensory organs, and with minds to relate to and understand these elements.

One cannot help but be impressed by the free and open words of affection these two lovers express toward each another. They do not play games with each other.

They do not suppress their real feelings out of some false sense of modesty. True, the woman defers to custom when she withholds public affection for her beloved (8:1). But elsewhere, her words and her actions clearly convey her feelings to her beloved. And likewise, he publicly celebrates his love for her. He prizes her beauty, he extols her virtue, and he praises her charms.

Song of Solomon sets a high standard for the expression of physical love. It pays tribute to the grandeur of sexuality without being pornographic. Sexuality complements a relationship of serious and mature love; in fact, loving sexuality is the intended design by which our species is continued. Sexuality is both natural and necessary, but it is to occur within the relational context of love.

§ § § § § § §

Song of Solomon 5–8

Introduction to These Chapters

These chapters may be outlined as follows.

The Missing Lover, II (5:2-8)

This section repeats the lost-lover motif employed earlier (3:1-5). However, here the maiden experiences reverse reprisal from the city watchmen. Even worse, she does not discover her missing lover, as she did in the earlier account.

In a dream the young maiden (bride) imagines that she awakens to the sounds of her lover knocking at the door outside the wall (verse 5). He pleads with her to open the door and allow him to enter her chamber. He claims that he is wet with dew. Unfortunately, the maiden has already bathed and dressed for bed and does not wish to become dirty. But her lover grasps the latch, ready to enter. The maiden hastens to turn the bolt, her hands dripping with perfume. When the door swings open, alas, her lover is not there. He has already gone. Frantically, she searches the city, calling him in vain. The watchmen find her, beat her, and strip her of her clothes. Finally, she pleads with the chorus, (her attendants, the *daughters of Jerusalem*), that when they find her missing lover, they remind him of her devoted love for him.

Closer examination of certain words and phrases in this story indicates that other meanings may be intended rather than the outward interpretation given above. The expressions *my head is wet (drenched) with dew* and *my locks (hair) with the drops (dampness) of the night* are probably references to male sex organs. In verses 4-5, the *latch (opening)* may refer to female sex organs and the *bolt (lock)* may indicate the male genitalia. The intense sexual overtones of this passage are not intended, however, for erotic excitement. Instead they function to intensify the atmosphere. Then, with the lover gone, the total sense of frustration of the maiden is clear to the readers. We are disappointed also! So the sexual imagery has a purpose other than sensuality. It contributes significantly to the total meaning of the story—the maiden's complete frustration with the untimely disappearance of her lover.

The Look of the Lover (5:9-16)

Verse 9 functions as an introduction to the graphic and figurative description the maiden offers of her beloved in verses 10-16. Presumably the questions are asked by the chorus, her attendants, the daughters of Jerusalem. Simply expressed, they want to know what is so special about her beloved. How is he different from other men?

The maiden answers their questions by providing an alluring picture of his physical attributes, his golden speech, and his incomparable attractiveness. Beginning with his head and moving downward over his body, she sketches impressions that convey images or thoughts rather than precise analogies. She is telling them what he means to her, the impact he makes on her, rather than explaining exactly how he appears.

His head is finely sculptured and elegantly poised on his shoulders; his hair is thick and black; his eyes are clear and dark, set against a white background; his bearded cheeks are kissed with fragrant scents; his arms are powerful yet tender; his entire body sparkles like precious gems; his legs are strong and broad. In sum, his looks are incomparable.

But even more appealing than his physical attributes is the lyrical quality of his speech. His words are a symphony, featuring love and charm. This is her beloved. *He is altogether desirable* (NRSV; NIV = *lovely*).

The Beloved Is Discovered (6:1-3)

Opening this section, the chorus joins in the search for the maiden's lost lover. Now that they understand how much he means to her, they willingly lend their aid.

With no reference to his apparent discovery and no element of transition, the maiden reports not only that she has found her lover, but that they are together in loving embraces. The allusion to a *garden* (verse 2) resumes a theme introduced earlier (4:12). The maiden and her beloved are together once again. He is pasturing his flock in the garden—among the lilies. This is probably a sexual reference, as in 2:16, but notice the care and openness with which the writer describes this experience. It is a holy moment, not a cheap thrill.

The Maiden's Extraordinary Beauty (6:4-10)

Once again the groom bursts forth in song proclaiming the incomparable beauty of his beloved maiden. His description of her (*beautiful as Tirzah, comely* (*lovely*) *as Jerusalem*) parallels the capital of Israel (the Northern Kingdom) with the capital of Judah (the Southern

Kingdom). This combination of cities dates to a time very early in the ninth century B.C., before King Omri abandoned Tirzah in favor of Samaria as his capital. Her beauty is awe-inspiring, like an army with banners; it is so overpowering that she must turn her mesmerizing gaze in another direction.

She radiates charm and grace. Her hair, her teeth, and her cheeks are described. She has an entourage of attractive female attendants, but this maiden, his beautiful beloved, stands out even among them. In fact, they too stand in awe of her beauty. She is the perfect daughter of her mother, flawed in no way. The song concludes with a rhetorical question, *Who is this that looks forth (appears) like the dawn?* Obviously, the correct response is the lovely maiden whom he loves.

The Nut Orchard (6:11-12)

The brief couplet is difficult to interpret, due to textual corruption in verse 12. Verse 11 describes the visit of the maiden to a nut garden to observe the blossoming of spring, with its fresh crop of fruit and nuts. Life has renewed itself, as love must do. Signs of fertility are all around. Assuming the wedding motif, the bride prepares herself for the beginning of marriage by a visit to an aphrodisiac garden. Her purpose is not inspection but empathetic identification with the coming of new life.

In Praise of the Shulammite Maiden (6:13–7:9)

A dance performed by the maiden evokes praise from her lover. He describes her physical attributes, beginning with her feet and moving upward. He eventually reaches her delicate and lovely mouth, just as earlier she described him beginning with his head and moving downward.

The identification of the maiden as a Shulammite is difficult to explain. Some scholars see in this name a reference to a Canaanite god worshiped in Jerusalem.

Other scholars propose that the expression is a feminine form of Solomon, suggesting *peace* or *wholeness*. Still others relate Shulammite to a village in Israel known as Shunen (see 1 Kings 1:3). In truth, the etymology is impossible to explain with any degree of certainty.

The expression *a dance before two armies* (NRSV; NIV = *the dance of Mahanaim*) may refer to an ancient rite relating to Israelite sacral warfare. While the specific references are vague in the opening command for the maiden to perform her dance, the old custom of a final dance by a bride before the groom and her attendants is well-attested in ancient Near Eastern social lore. As her wedding celebration nears its end, the bride does a final dance.

The bridegroom is enthralled with her performance. He is so pleased, in fact, that he again breaks out in lavish praise for her. As earlier (4:1-7; 6:4-10), his words communicate impressions rather than precise analogies. Beginning with her feet wrapped in sandals, he moves slowly upward selecting particularly important features to highlight. Her thighs are carefully and delicately formed—all in proper proportion; her navel is round and deep—suggesting health and fecundity; her stomach is embroidered with lilies and sprouting wheat—the source of sensuality and abundance. He finally reaches her head, by way of her lovely breasts. He confesses that her kisses are like fine wine.

To compare his beloved with a stately palm tree is a rare compliment indeed. The palm tree is a classical sex symbol in the ancient world; it inspires sexual fertility, just as his Shulammite maiden emits sensuality. The erotic language is powerful and effective here, but not degrading or pornographic. The king (verse 5) is overwrought by his feelings, and his ardent desire for his beloved maiden excites him to passion. The thoughts of climbing the tree and laying hold of its branches are certainly euphemisms for intimacy. True love is passionate love.

Love in the Garden (7:10-13)

In response (presumably) to her lover's ardent affection for her, the maiden invites him to accompany her to a country vineyard. Obviously, the season is spring and the vineyard is filled with new fruit. The sexual motif is very evident here, as the maiden promises to give her love to her beloved. Grapes, pomegranates, and mandrakes are all delicacies suggestive of aphrodisiacs and fertility rites. This is truly an invitation he cannot refuse.

Love in the Chamber (8:1-4)

In this brief poem, the maiden longs for the freedom to express her love openly for her beloved. She wishes that he were like a brother to her, then she could kiss him publicly without incurring general condemnation. Public displays of affection were frowned upon in ancient Israel, and perhaps unfairly, it was always the woman who suffered public disdain. However, if the object of her display of affection were a relative (8:1), then public censure would be less severe. Unfortunately, however, this is not the case, and she must control her ardor.

Unlike the existential reality in 3:4, in this flight of her fantasy in chapter 8 she can only dream of leading him into her love-chamber. She has romantic images of what it would be like—drinking spiced wine, sipping the aphrodisiacal nectar of pomegranates. And then they would unite in a blissful moment of love (verse 3). As earlier in 3:5, she asks her attendants to leave them undisturbed until they have sated themselves with love.

The Strength of Love (8:5-7)

Verse 5a probably refers back to 4:16 and 6:2, where the wedding couple retire to a beautiful garden to consummate their love amid signs of life and new birth. Here, perhaps, the allusion is to their return from that garden. She leans upon the shoulder of her beloved; both are exhausted from love. Other scholars interpret this passage as referring to the emergence from the underworld of the god and goddess, to accompany the arrival of spring.

Verse 5b seems out of place in both its theme and its structure. This is the first (and only) reference to the groom's mother. The apple tree may function here as a fertility symbol.

Verses 6-8 celebrate the incomparable worth of love. The maiden urges her lover (now her husband) to honor their new union much the same as he honors his seal, which he wears upon his hand or about his neck. Since writing ability was scarce, most men carried seals as identification and for signature purposes. Also, the inscription on the seal usually signified something about the person. So, the maiden now asks her new husband for constancy and companionship—to be together always. The seal is a symbol of identity; the maiden's love requires the same honor.

Love, she says, is as strong as death, more vivid than fire, and more resilient to flood. Truly, love is worth far more than any wealth or other possession. Such a powerful love should not be taken lightly, she implies, for it is a treasure beyond all price. What person would not eagerly scorn great wealth for mature and serious love? No one!

The Maiden Cares for Herself (8:8-10)

Scholarly interpretation of these three verses ranges from humorous and sarcastic to preservation of the maiden's chastity. It is difficult to relate these verses to this book in particular or to love poetry in general. Whether the speakers are truly *brothers* (as in 1:6) or whether this is a euphemism for other lovers is unclear.

Possibly this section is a flashback by the maiden to her childhood when she came beneath her family's fraternal arm. What were her brothers' obligations to her? How were they to help her—by increasing her dowry (*a battlement* [*towers*] *of silver*) and by protecting her from harm (*with boards* [*panels*] *of cedar*)? She is their responsibility. They honor the trust bestowed upon them.

But, as she matured, she became a wealth unto herself and did not need their help and protection. She grew up physically and socially, and found a perfect suitor to complement her identity. She needed no help from her brothers. She cared for herself.

Solomon's Vineyard (8:11-12)

This brief vignette espouses the idea that love is the exclusive privilege of the beloved. Although thematically unrelated to the context, this addition makes a valuable point. The story is told of how King Solomon owned a vineyard at Baal-hamon. He leased it for a high price to various tenants. They paid for its use, and retained a portion of the profits. By contrast, his (the beloved's) vineyard (namely his wife), he proclaims, is his very own! A valuable wife (vineyard) is not to be shared, no matter how high the lease price. The parallelism between wife and vineyard is very prevalent in oriental love poetry.

Conclusion: Call and Response (8:13-14)

The book concludes with a final couplet constituting a call and response. Verse 13 is a call by the lover to his maiden. Obviously, she has hidden herself within the garden, possibly as part of the marriage celebration. The groom and his guests must now search for her.

She responds, inviting her husband to come quickly to her. The *gazelle* and *stag* appear elsewhere (2:17) as symbols of strength and virility. Spice-laden mountains is an allusion intended to strengthen the sexual desire of her lover, as it would increase the virility of the gazelle and the stag. Once the game of "hide and seek" has ended the lovers can hold each other close.

§ § § § § § §

The Message of Song of Solomon 5–8

Continuing human love is the primary focus of the book. Serious students will discover that human sexuality, while important, is not the only factor in the relationship of love. Serious and mature love, as exists between the king and his beautiful bride, entails fidelity. In 8:6-7, the maiden enjoins her husband to wear her as a seal about his arm and around his neck. Love has bound them together, and each has a claim of fidelity upon the other.

A strong marriage is nurtured by faithfulness of both partners. They will neither need nor want an affectionate relationship with another person. As the maiden says in 8:6, *love is as strong as death*. A sense of fidelity dissipates the danger of jealousy. The bonds of love bind the relationship together so tightly that none can break it apart. As seen in 6:3, *I am my beloved's and my beloved is mine* (NRSV; NIV = *I am my lover's and my lover is mine*).

Serious and mature love is nurtured also by a deep concern for the well-being of each other. The "missing lover" theme may have been part of the ritual or wedding love that prompted some of these songs. But the distress of the maiden at the sudden and inexplicable disappearance of her beloved reflects her genuine concern. Her sense of loneliness and concern override her fear of danger at night, as she frantically searches for him throughout the city.

Even when she is victimized (5:7) by the watchmen, she does not waver in her concern for her beloved. She urges her attendants to continue the search and, when they find him, to assure him of her love.

Third, it is abundantly clear from their song that the maiden has reserved her most intimate affections for her husband. She has not been promiscuous. He describes her garden as locked and her fountain as sealed (4:12). In 7:13, the fruits she has stored likely refer to her sexuality. In every respect, this beautiful and stately maiden has not allowed herself to be used, opting instead to wait and reserve her deepest expressions of love for one who truly honors them.

Fourth, serious and mature love between two adults is fully reciprocal. It is clear that both persons are deeply attracted to each other. Their feelings are mutual, and their trust invites open and free expression of this love. Each one offers praise and respect for the other. Each one finds joy in the other's embrace. Each one longs for that special moment of union, when they become as one in sexual embrace. There is no doubt in the mind of one as to the feelings or motives of the other.

§ § § § § § §

Glossary of Terms

Abaddon: This term is an alternative name for Sheol, the realm of the dead. It is a dark and cheerless place where one mostly sleeps.

Agur: An anonymous figure in Proverbs 30:1-9 who questions the limits and possibilities of human knowledge.

Amana: A very high mountain in southern Lebanon.

Amenemopet: An Egyptian author whose collection of instructions served as a source for Proverbs 22:17–24:22.

Bath-rabbim: An entrance to Heshbon; possibly a gate where there was a pool of water nearby.

Carmel: A relatively high mountain on the western coast of Israel, near modern Haifa.

Damascus: The capital of Syria in ancient times as well as today.

En-gedi: A spring-fed oasis approximately halfway down the western side of the Dead Sea. This site was an extremely important military outpost and source of water for Judean shepherds.

Eternity: A Hebrew term used by Qoheleth in 3:11 to indicate the mystery persons sense about God's plan or the meaning of the world.

Folly: A term used by the sages who wrote Proverbs to describe actions that willfully ignore moral virtue or the natural laws.

Gilead: The name of a tribe and/or territory east of the

Jordan River. It contains well-forested hills watered by several streams and springs.

Hermon: A mountain situated north of Israel in southern Lebanon, approximately 9,000 feet high.

Heshbon: A city across the Jordan River from Israel in Moab.

Hezekiah: An important king of Judah from 715-686 B.C. Some of his royal scribes were active in the preservation and transmission of Proverbs.

Kedar: Arabian bedouin tribes well known for their black goat's hair tents.

Lemuel: A young ruler (or king) whose mother offers him advice on the behavior of kings in Proverbs 31:1-9.

Palanquin: A litter, frequently enclosed and used to transport royalty, especially at festive occasions.

Proverb: A two-line saying that uses parallelism to teach a moral lesson or register an observation about the world.

Redeemer: This term refers to one who is responsible for covering the debts of a kinsman or for avenging the death of a family member. Ruth 4:4-6 is a good example of this concept.

Righteousness: A term used by the sages to describe proper moral conduct; also used to designate fairness and fulfillment of contractual obligations.

Senir: In Deuteronomy 3:9, this Amorite term is used to refer to Mount Hermon. The Amorites were probably ancestors of the Hebrews, or at least used a similar language.

Sharon: A coastal plain extending from central Palestine northward to Mount Carmel. This was an important agricultural region in ancient Israel.

Sheol: A term that refers to the realm of the dead. In Hebrew thought all deceased persons went there.

Shulammite: The term is of uncertain origin. It refers to the wife of the king in Song of Solomon who danced before her husband following their marriage. See the commentary on 6:13.

Tirzah: A city in northern Israel that served as capital until King Omri relocated it at Samaria.

Vanity: A term used by Qoheleth to describe the meaninglessness of human existence.

Wisdom: A term applied to superior intelligence, enabling one to achieve moral insight leading to righteousness.

Guide to Pronunciation

Abaddon: AH-ba-don
Agur: AH-gur
Amana: Ah-MAH-nah
Amenemopet: Ah-men-EM-oh-pay
Bath-rabbim: Bah-AHTH-rah-BEEM
Carmel: Car-MEL
Damascus: Duh-MASK-us
En-gedi: En-GED-dee
Gilead: GIH-lee-ad
Hermon: Her-MON
Heshbon: HESH-bon
Hezekiah: Heh-zeh-KIGH-ah
Kedar: KAY-dar
Lemuel: LEM-you-el
Palanquin: PAL-an-keen
Senir: Seh-NEER
Sheol: Sheh-OLE
Shulammite: SHOO-lah-mite
Tirzah: TEER-zah